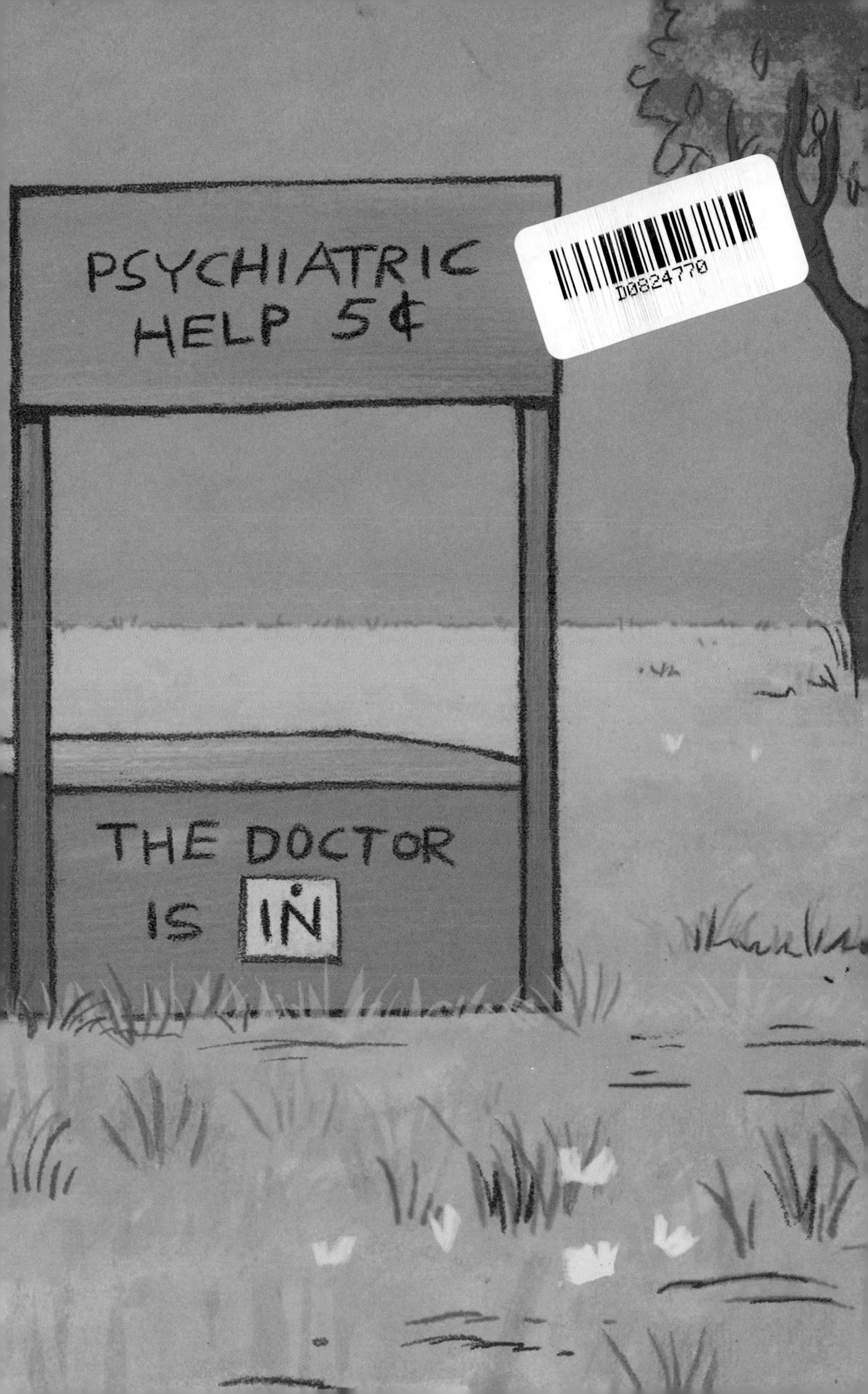
PSYCHIATRIC
HELP 5¢
THE DOCTOR
IS IN

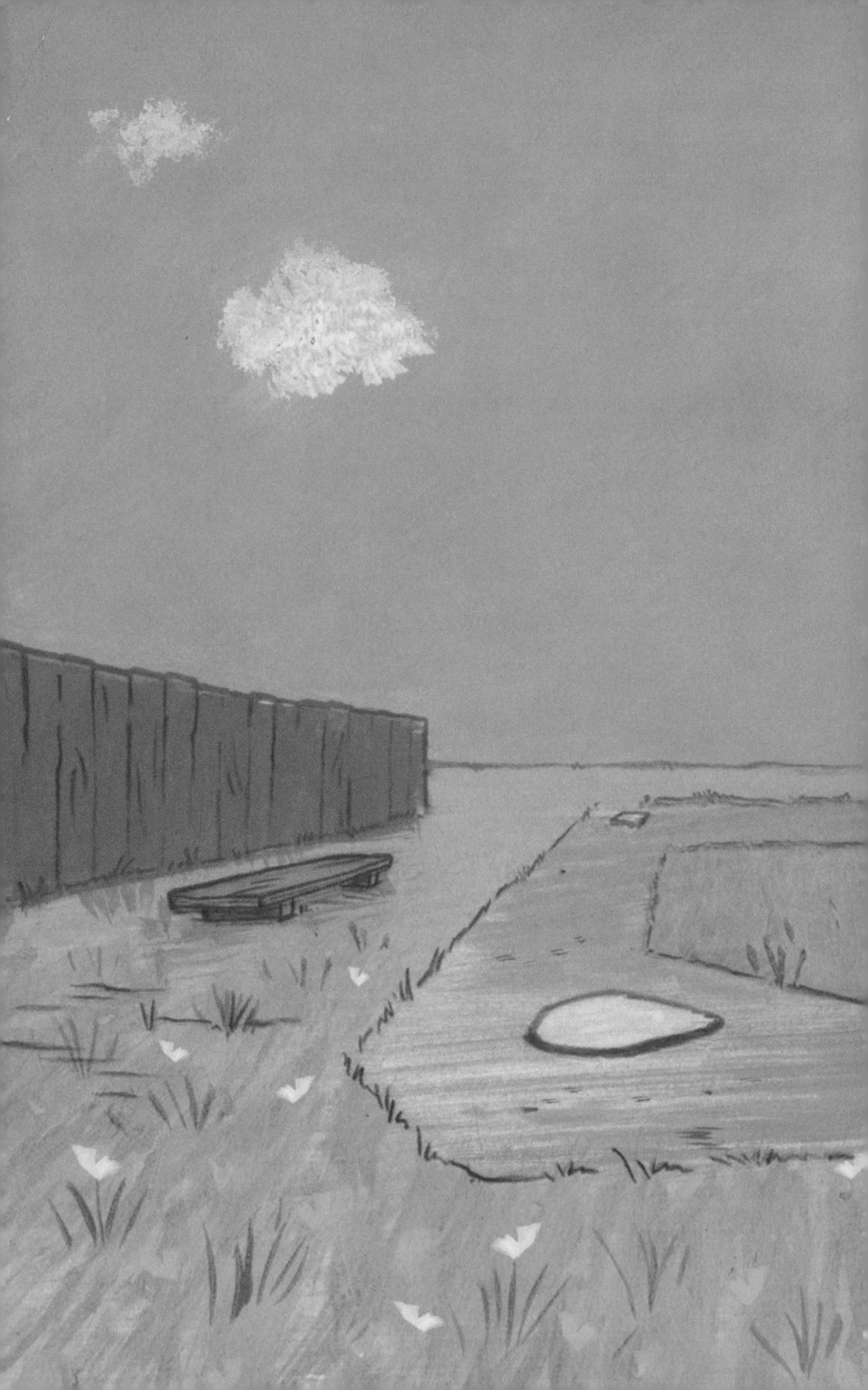

Charles M. Schulz

PEANUTS™

Happiness is a Warm Blanket, Charlie Brown!

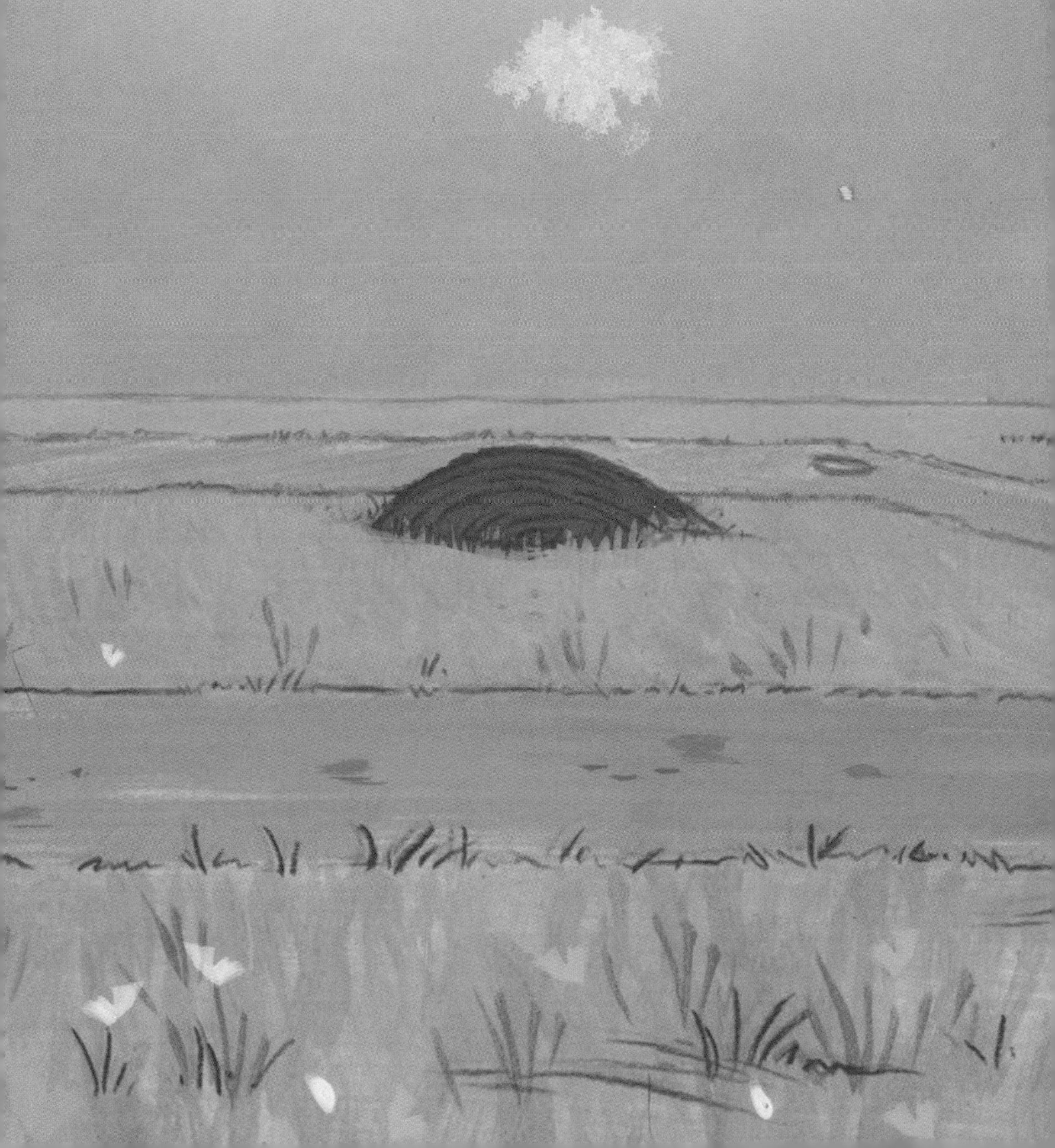

Ross Richie - Chief Executive Officer
Matt Gagnon - Editor-in-Chief
Adam Fortier - VP-New Business
Wes Harris - VP-Publishing
Lance Kreiter - VP-Licensing & Merchandising
Chip Mosher - Marketing Director

Bryce Carlson - Managing Editor
Ian Brill - Editor
Dafna Pleban - Editor
Christopher Burns - Editor
Christopher Meyer - Editor
Shannon Watters - Assistant Editor
Eric Harburn - Assistant Editor
Adam Staffaroni - Assistant Editor

Neil Loughrie - Publishing Coordinator
Brian Latimer - Lead Graphic Designer
Stephanie Gonzaga - Graphic Designer
Travis Beaty - Traffic Coordinator
Ivan Salazar - Marketing Assistant
Brett Grinnell - Executive Assistant

A catalog record of this book is available from OCLC and from the BOOM! Studios website, www.boom-studios.com, on the Librarians Page. Manufactured by Friesens Corportation in Altona, MB, Canada (March 2011) Job #64193.

kaboom!, 6310 San Vicente Boulevard, Suite 107, Los Angeles, CA 90048-5457. Printed in Canada. First Printing. ISBN: 978-1-60886-682-3

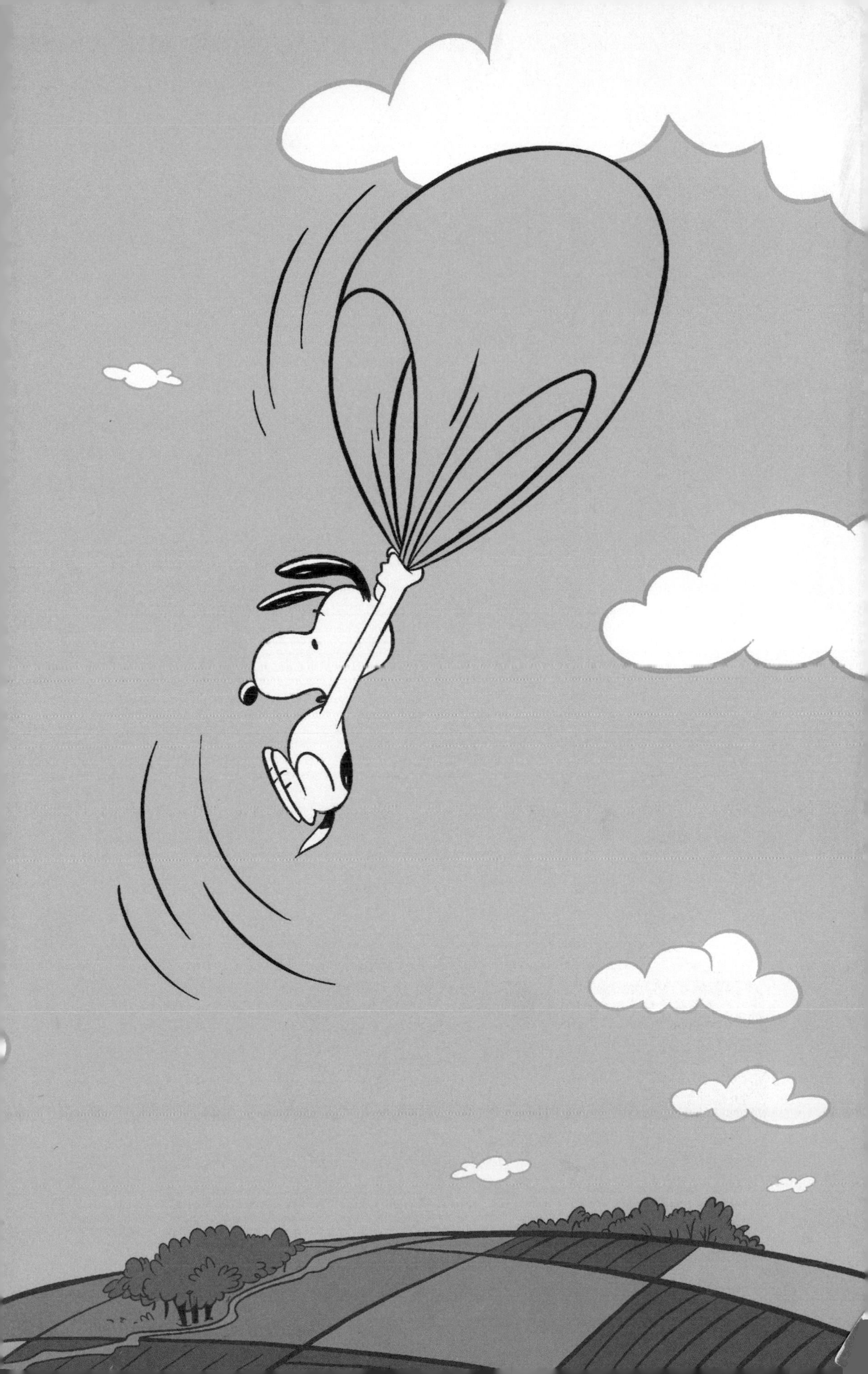

Based on the comic strip by
Charles M. Schulz

ADAPTED BY:

SCRIPT:
Stephan Pastis and Craig Schulz

ART DIRECTION:
Paige Braddock and Andy Beall

LAYOUTS:
Vicki Scott

PENCILS:
Bob Scott and Vicki Scott

INKS:
Ron Zorman

COLORS:
Brian Miller, Hi-Fi Colour Design

COVER:
Bob Scott

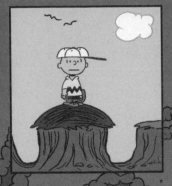

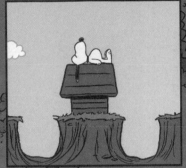

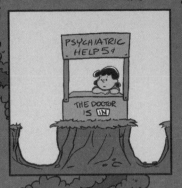

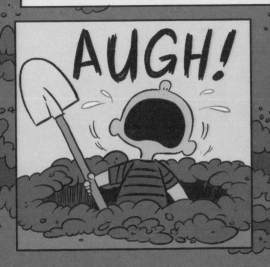

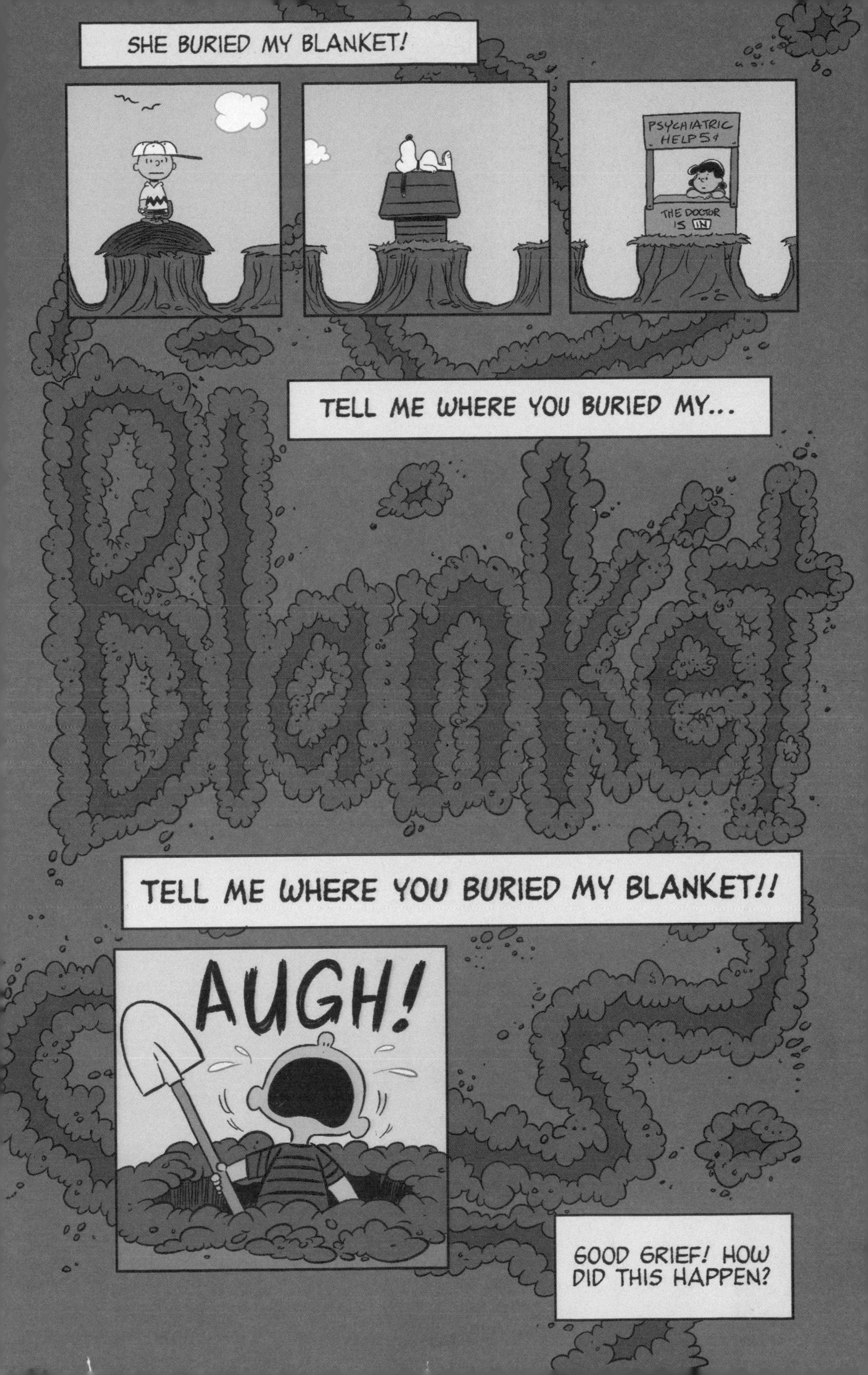
SHE BURIED MY BLANKET!
PSYCHIATRIC HELP 5¢
THE DOCTOR IS IN
TELL ME WHERE YOU BURIED MY...
Blanket
TELL ME WHERE YOU BURIED MY BLANKET!!
AUGH!
GOOD GRIEF! HOW DID THIS HAPPEN?

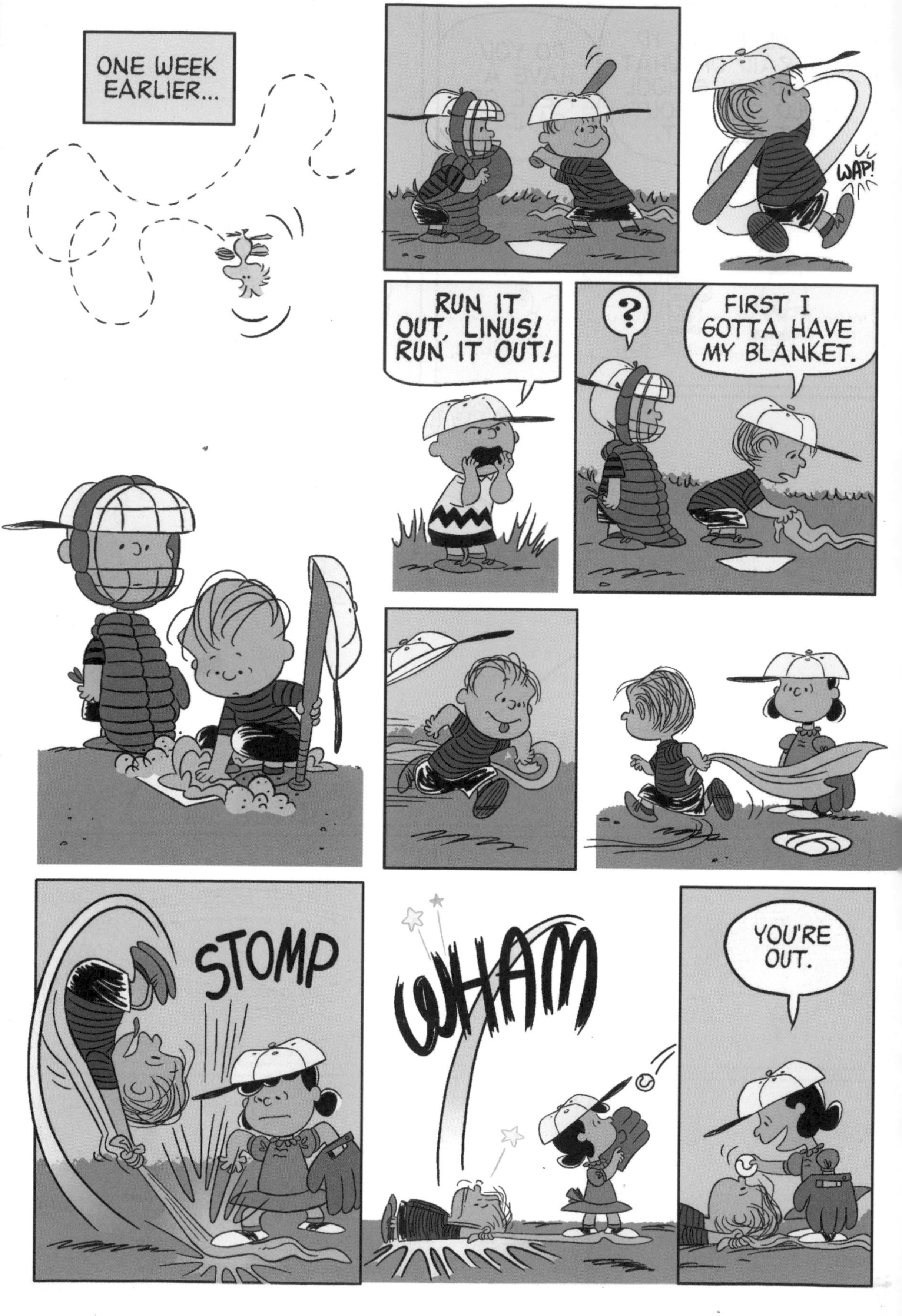
ONE WEEK EARLIER...
WAP!
RUN IT OUT, LINUS! RUN IT OUT!
?
FIRST I GOTTA HAVE MY BLANKET.
STOMP
WHAM
YOU'RE OUT.

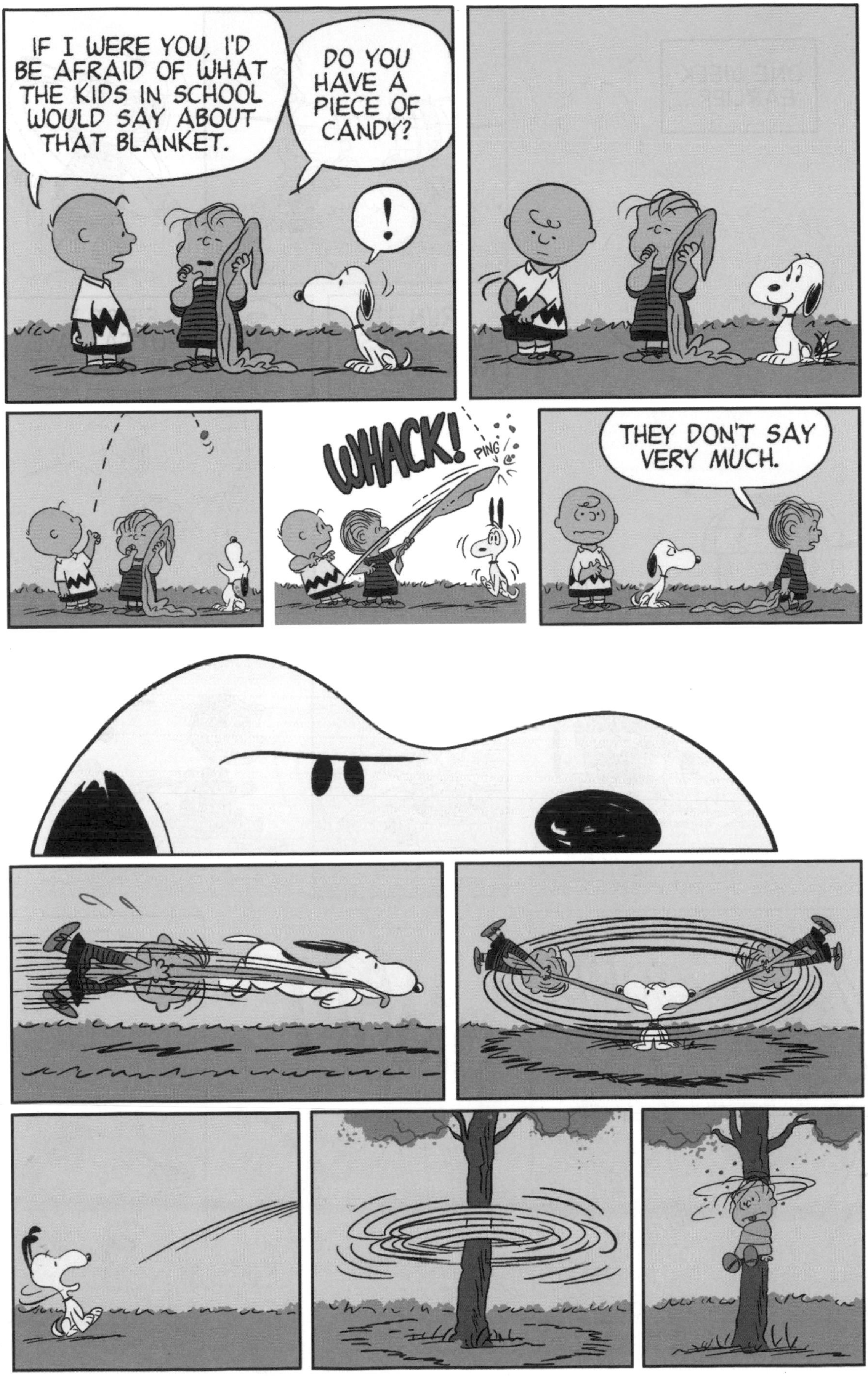
IF I WERE YOU, I'D BE AFRAID OF WHAT THE KIDS IN SCHOOL WOULD SAY ABOUT THAT BLANKET.
DO YOU HAVE A PIECE OF CANDY?
!
WHACK!
PING
THEY DON'T SAY VERY MUCH.

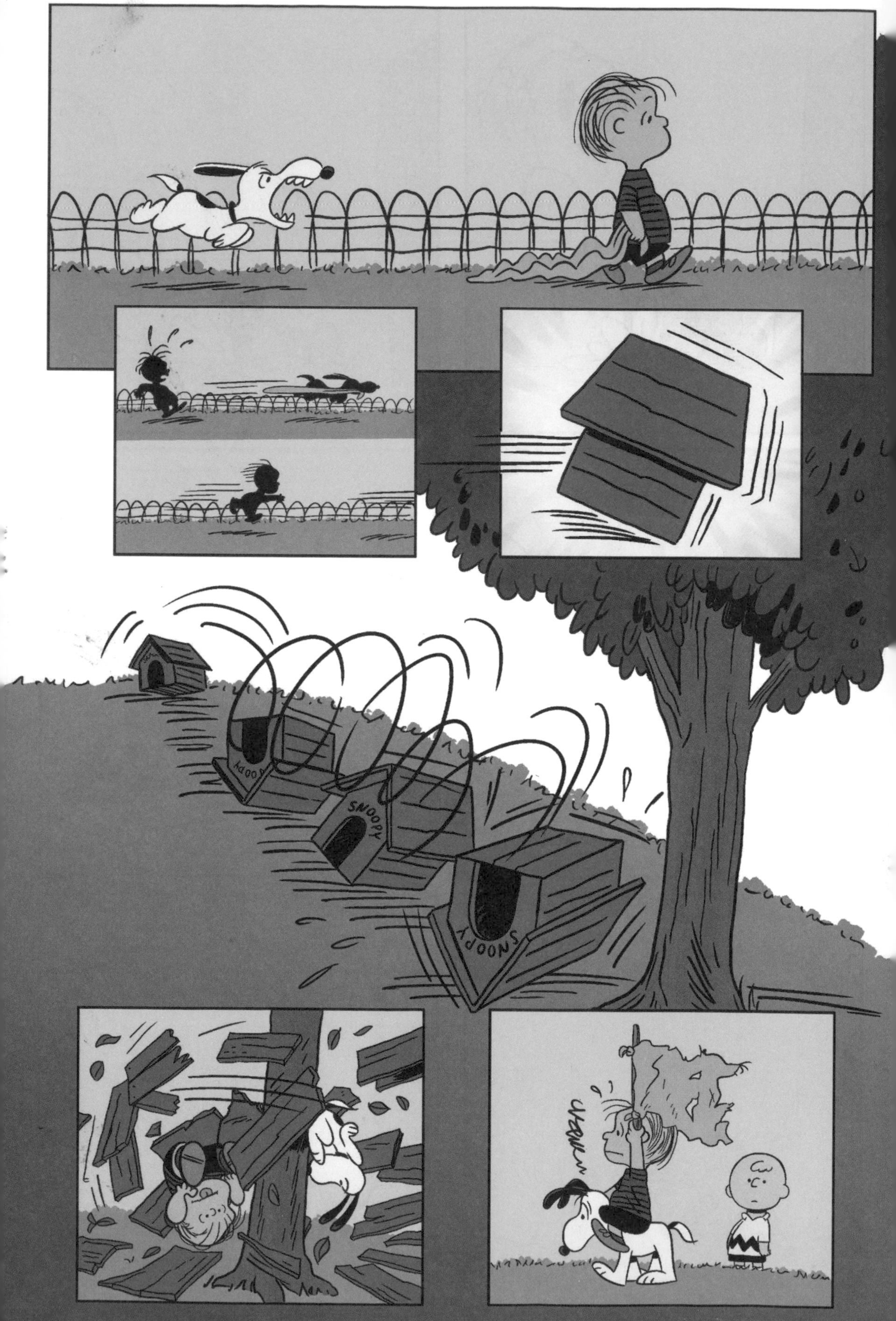
SNOOPY
SNOOPY
SNOOPY

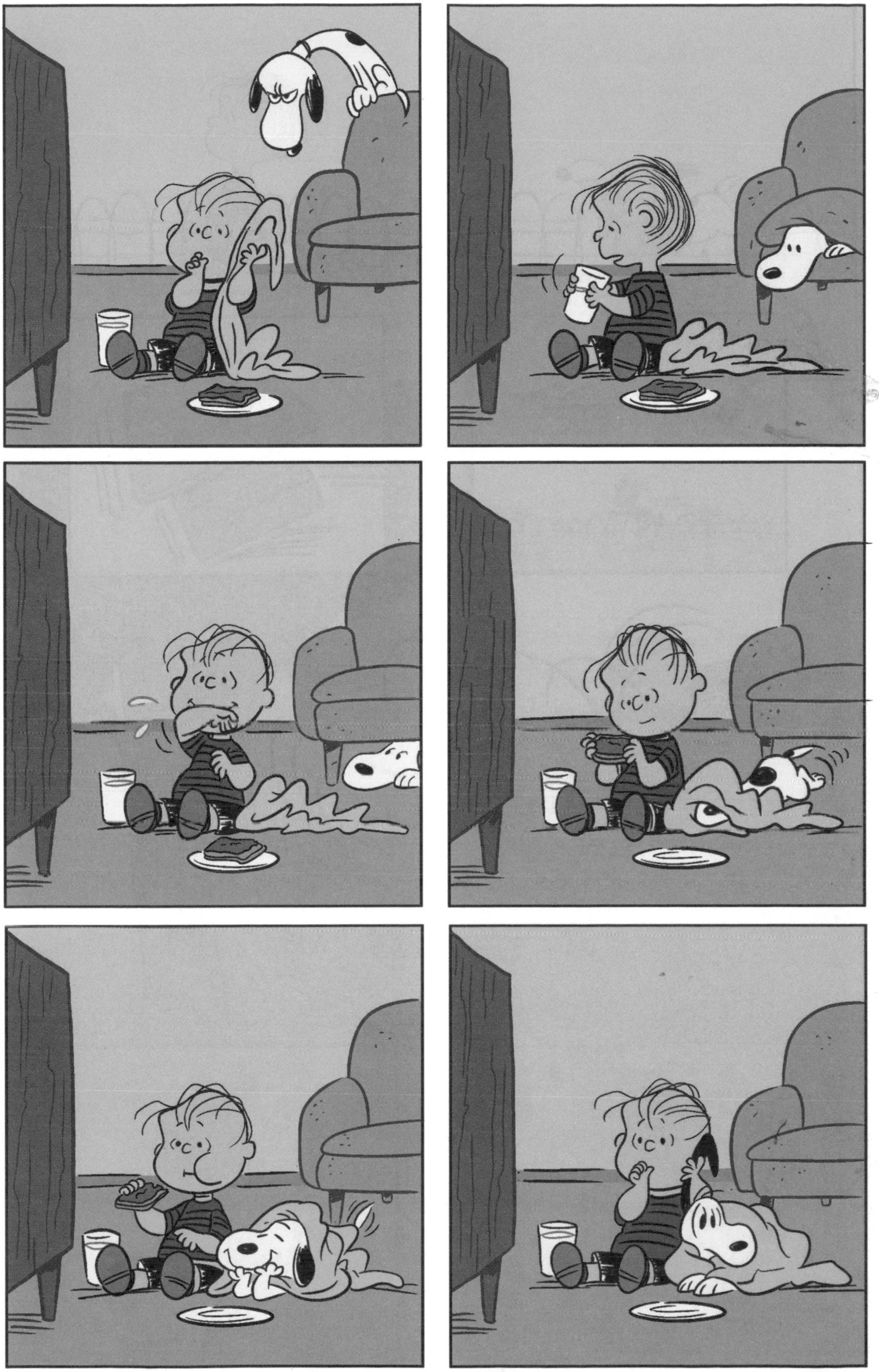

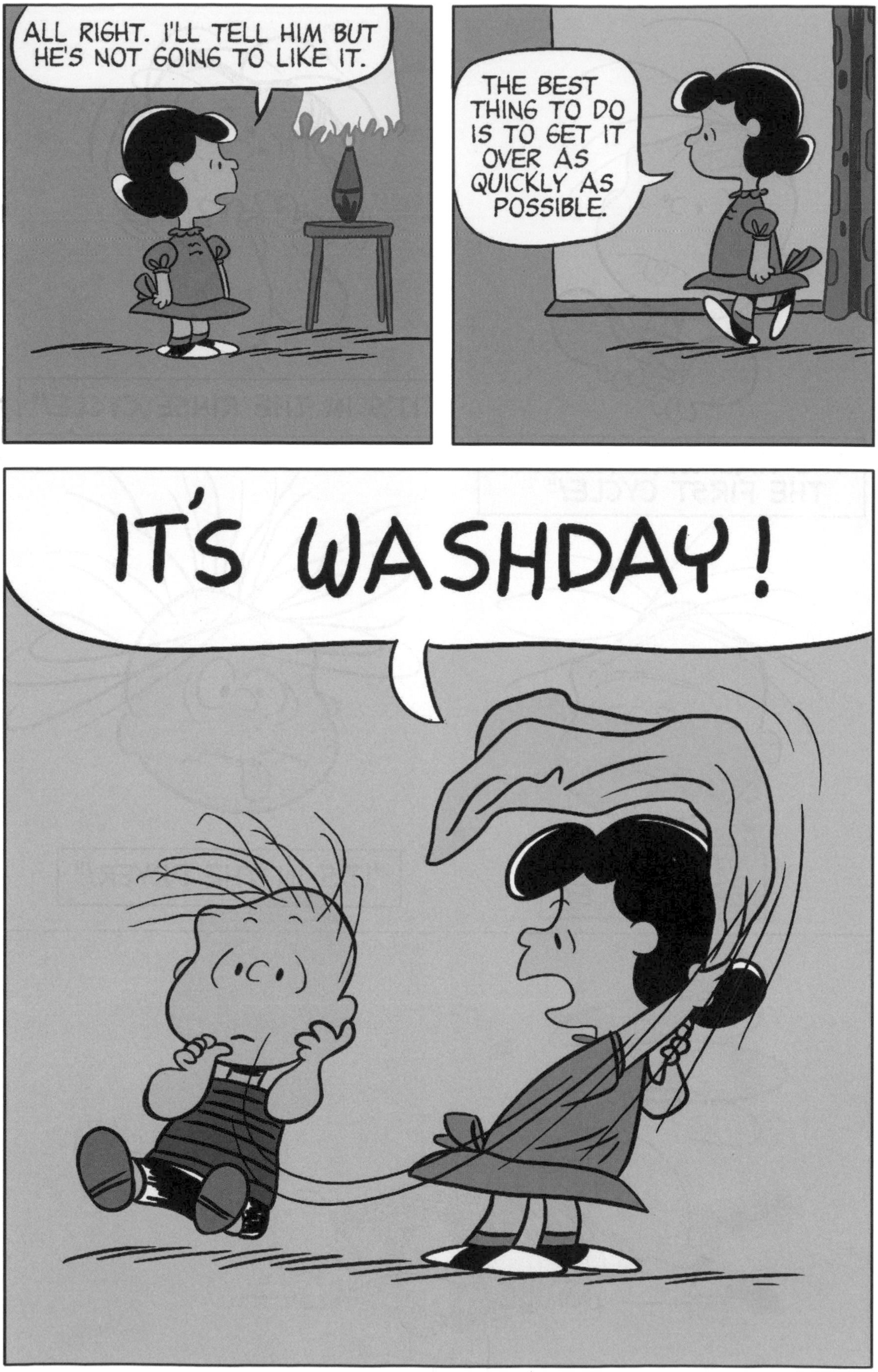
ALL RIGHT. I'LL TELL HIM BUT HE'S NOT GOING TO LIKE IT.
THE BEST THING TO DO IS TO GET IT OVER AS QUICKLY AS POSSIBLE.
IT'S WASHDAY!

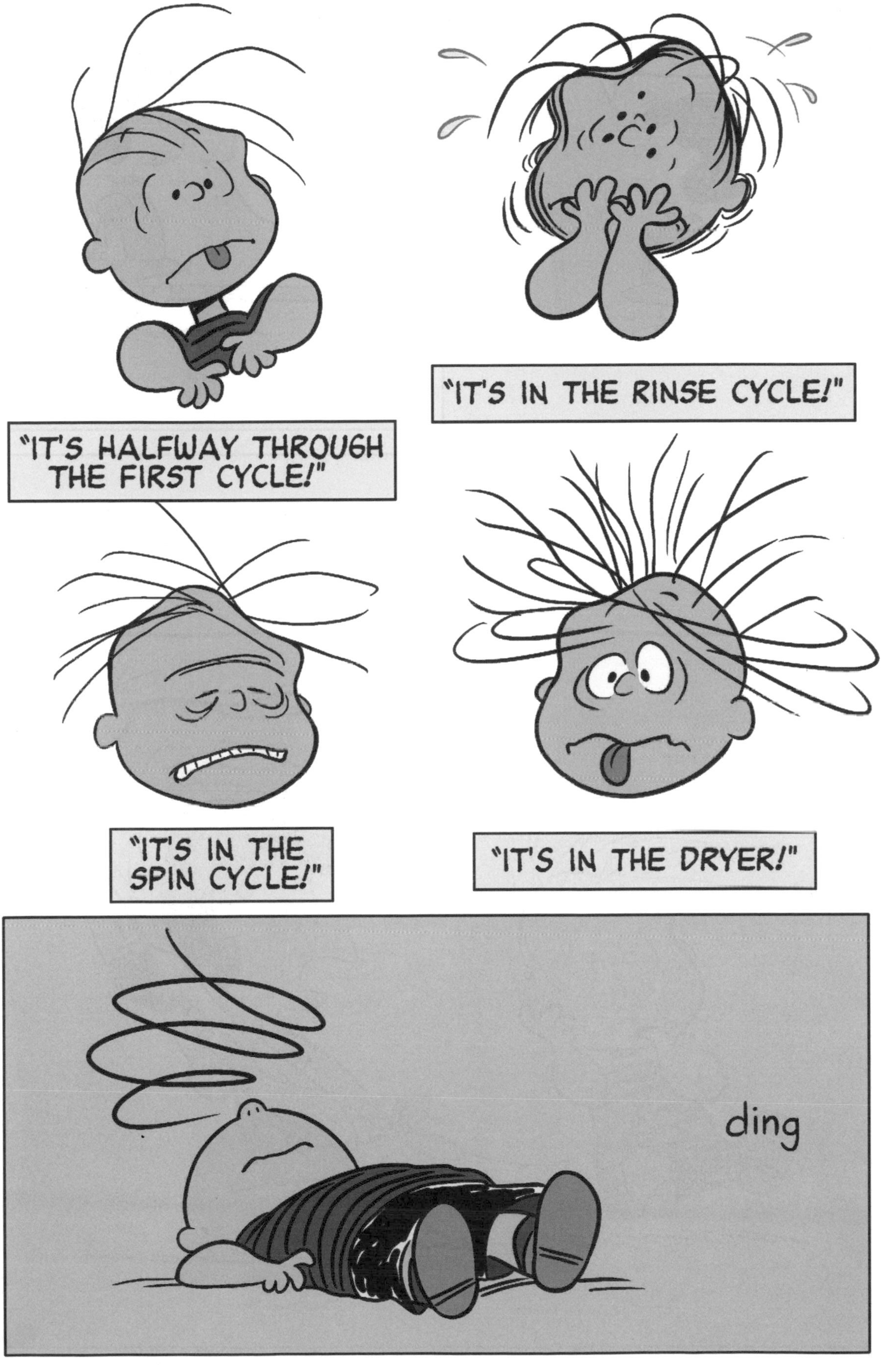
"IT'S HALFWAY THROUGH THE FIRST CYCLE!"
"IT'S IN THE RINSE CYCLE!"
"IT'S IN THE SPIN CYCLE!"
"IT'S IN THE DRYER!"
ding

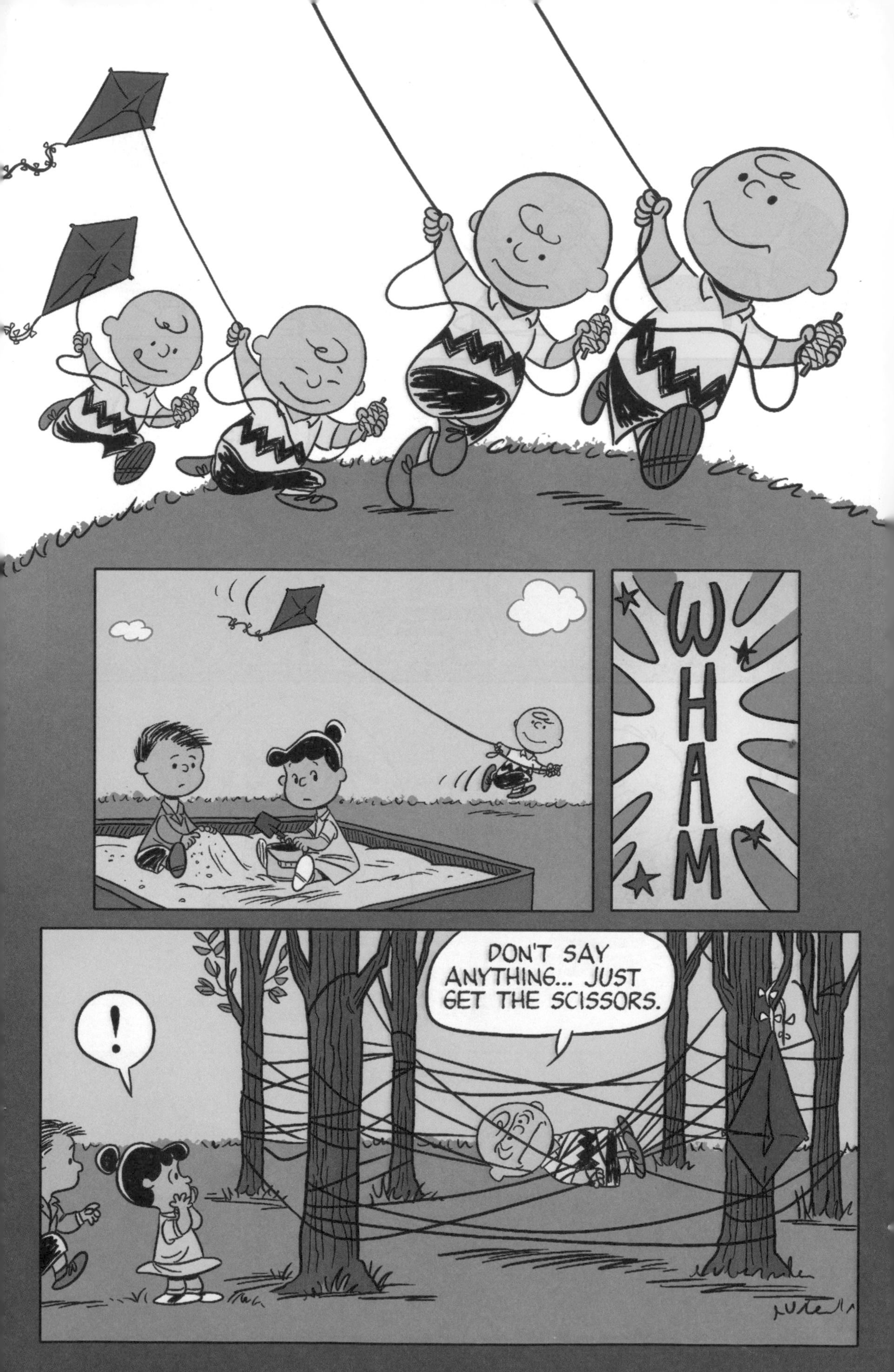

WHAM
!
DON'T SAY ANYTHING... JUST GET THE SCISSORS.

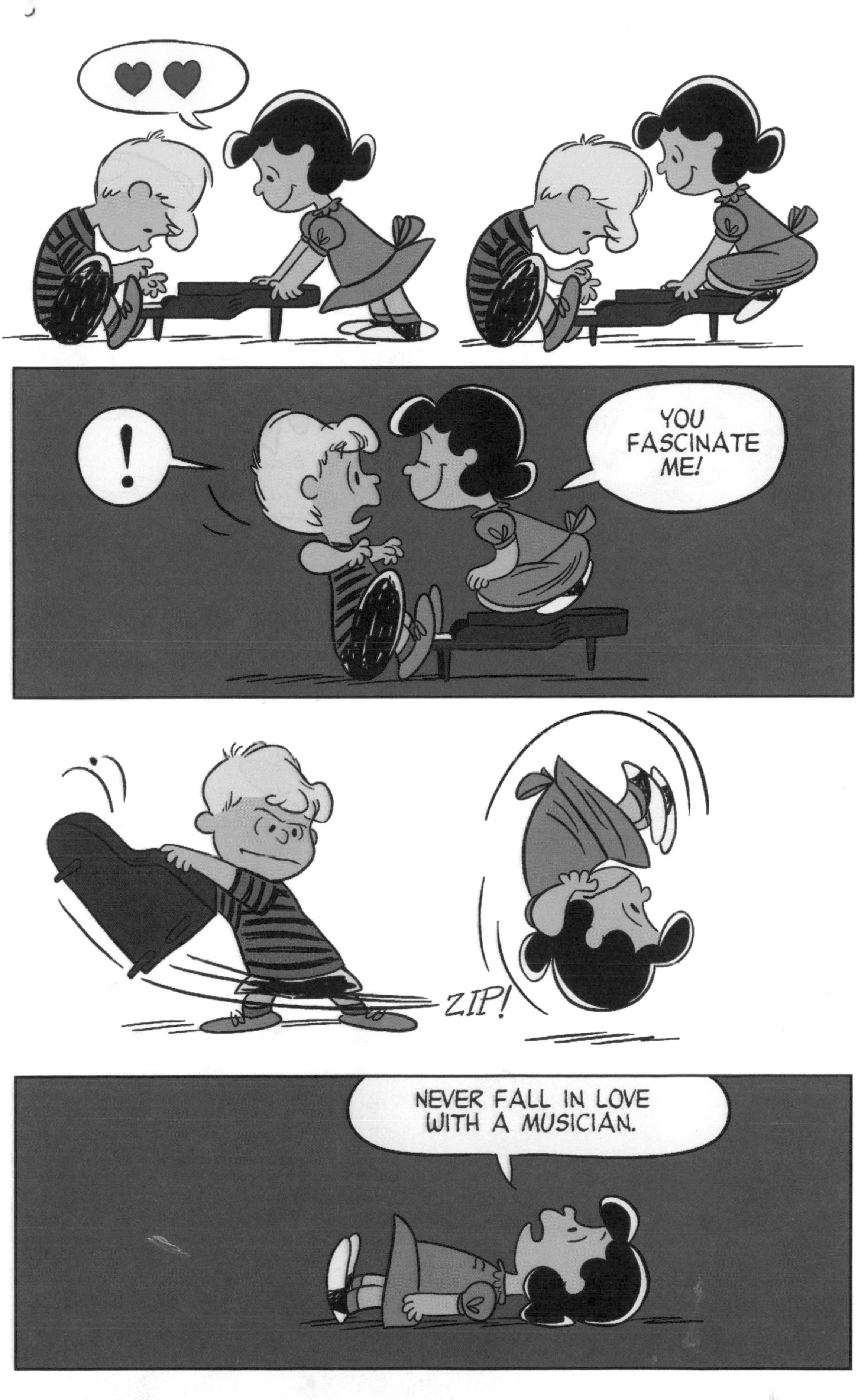

!
YOU FASCINATE ME!
ZIP!
NEVER FALL IN LOVE WITH A MUSICIAN.

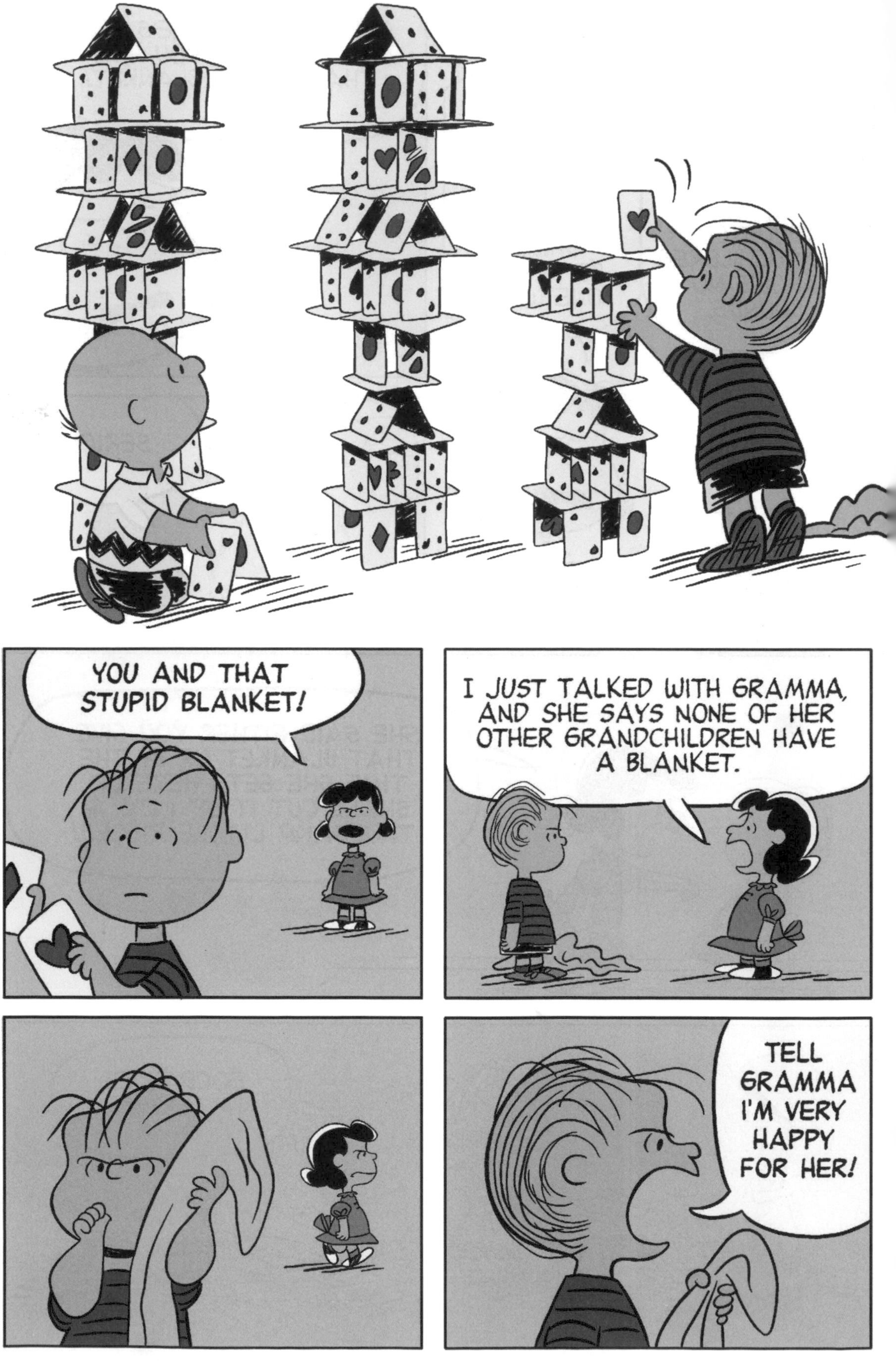
YOU AND THAT STUPID BLANKET!
I JUST TALKED WITH GRAMMA, AND SHE SAYS NONE OF HER OTHER GRANDCHILDREN HAVE A BLANKET.
TELL GRAMMA I'M VERY HAPPY FOR HER!

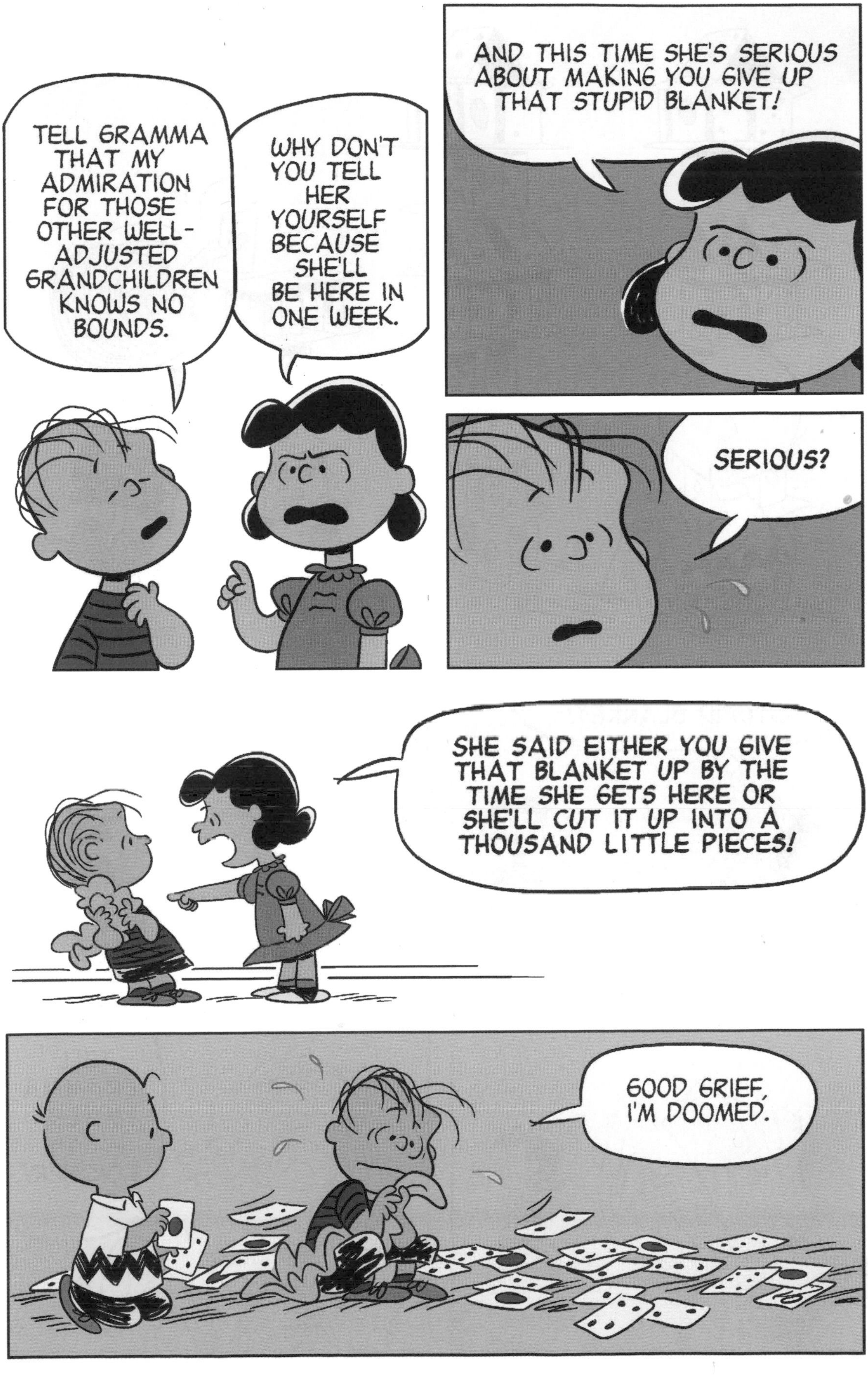
TELL GRAMMA THAT MY ADMIRATION FOR THOSE OTHER WELL-ADJUSTED GRANDCHILDREN KNOWS NO BOUNDS.
WHY DON'T YOU TELL HER YOURSELF BECAUSE SHE'LL BE HERE IN ONE WEEK.
AND THIS TIME SHE'S SERIOUS ABOUT MAKING YOU GIVE UP THAT STUPID BLANKET!
SERIOUS?
SHE SAID EITHER YOU GIVE THAT BLANKET UP BY THE TIME SHE GETS HERE OR SHE'LL CUT IT UP INTO A THOUSAND LITTLE PIECES!
GOOD GRIEF, I'M DOOMED.

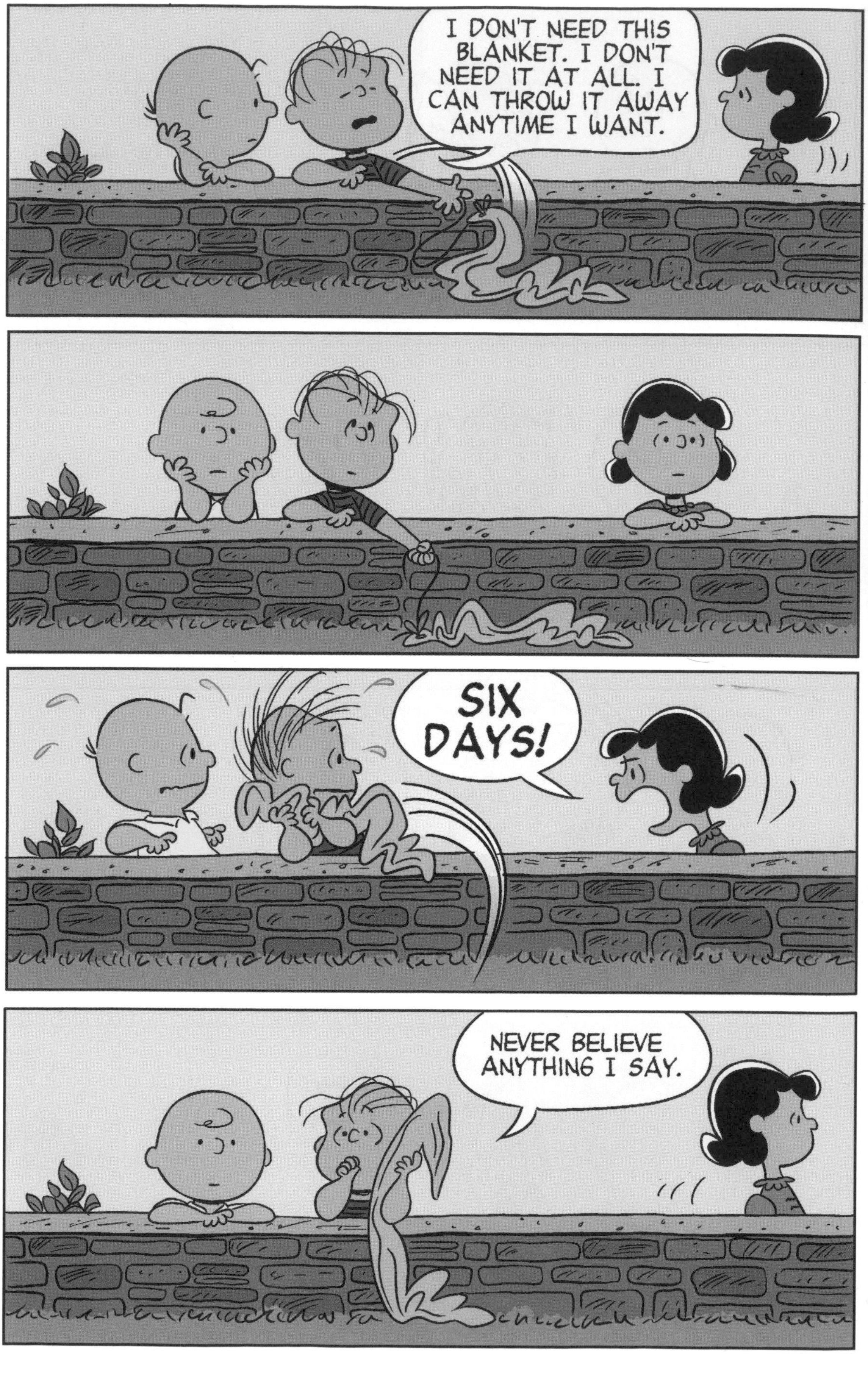
I DON'T NEED THIS BLANKET. I DON'T NEED IT AT ALL. I CAN THROW IT AWAY ANYTIME I WANT.
SIX DAYS!
NEVER BELIEVE ANYTHING I SAY.

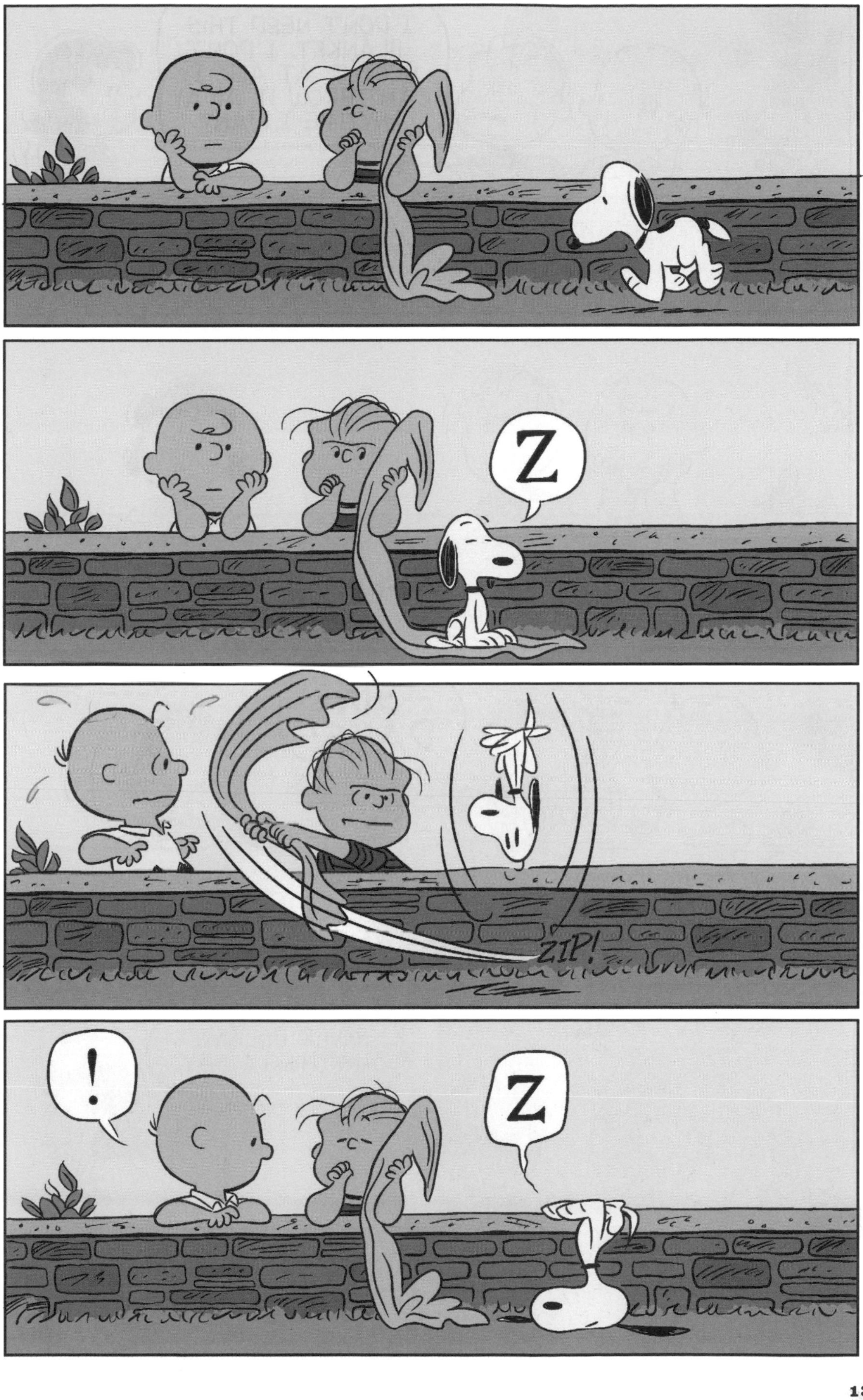

Z
ZIP!
!
Z

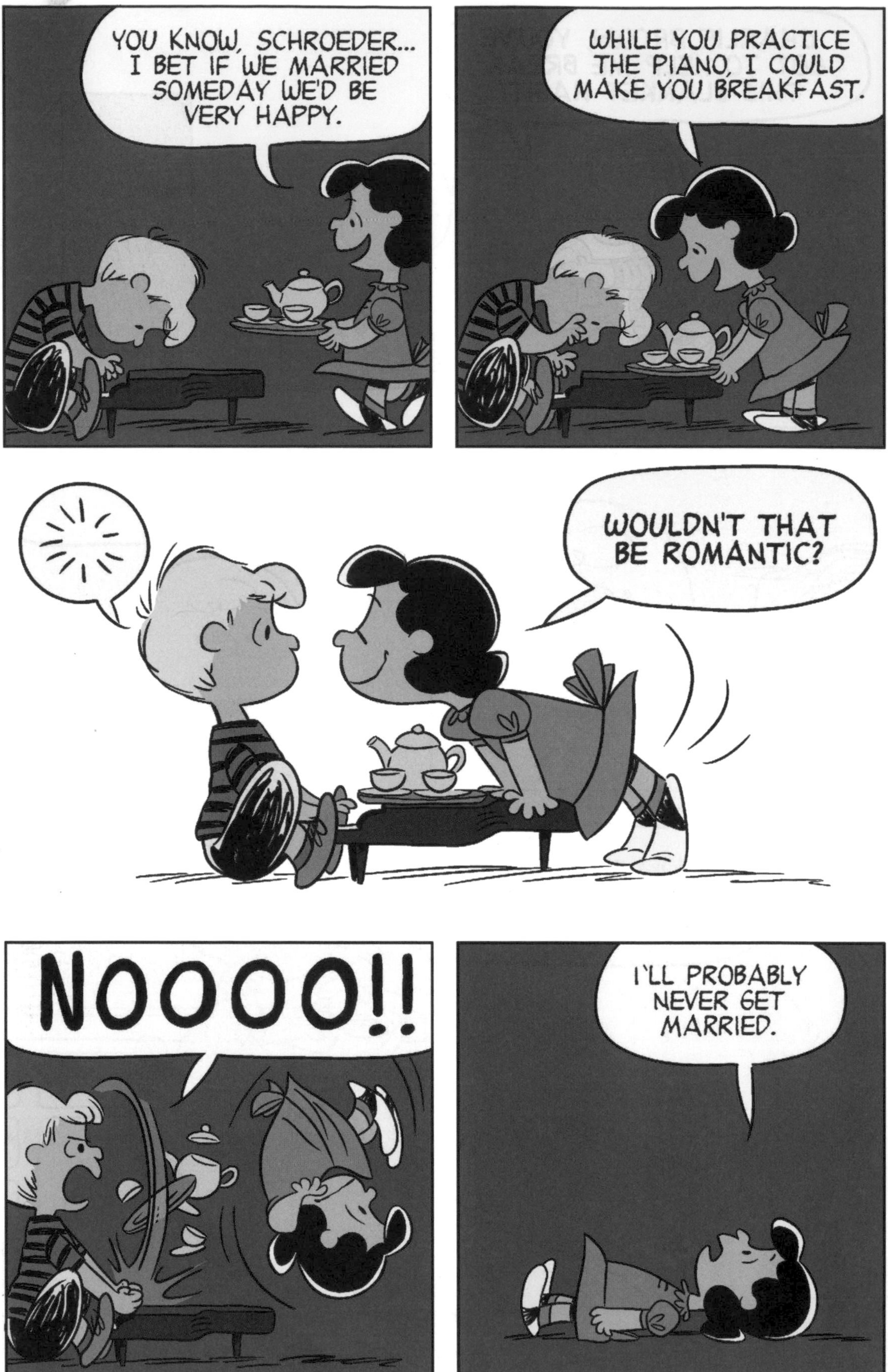
YOU KNOW, SCHROEDER... I BET IF WE MARRIED SOMEDAY WE'D BE VERY HAPPY.
WHILE YOU PRACTICE THE PIANO, I COULD MAKE YOU BREAKFAST.
WOULDN'T THAT BE ROMANTIC?
NOOOO!!
I'LL PROBABLY NEVER GET MARRIED.

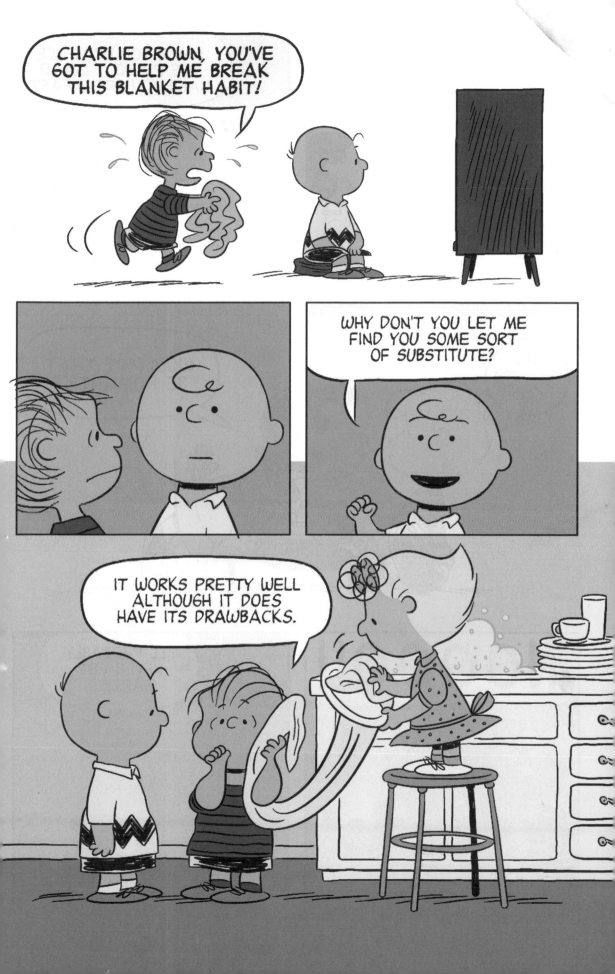

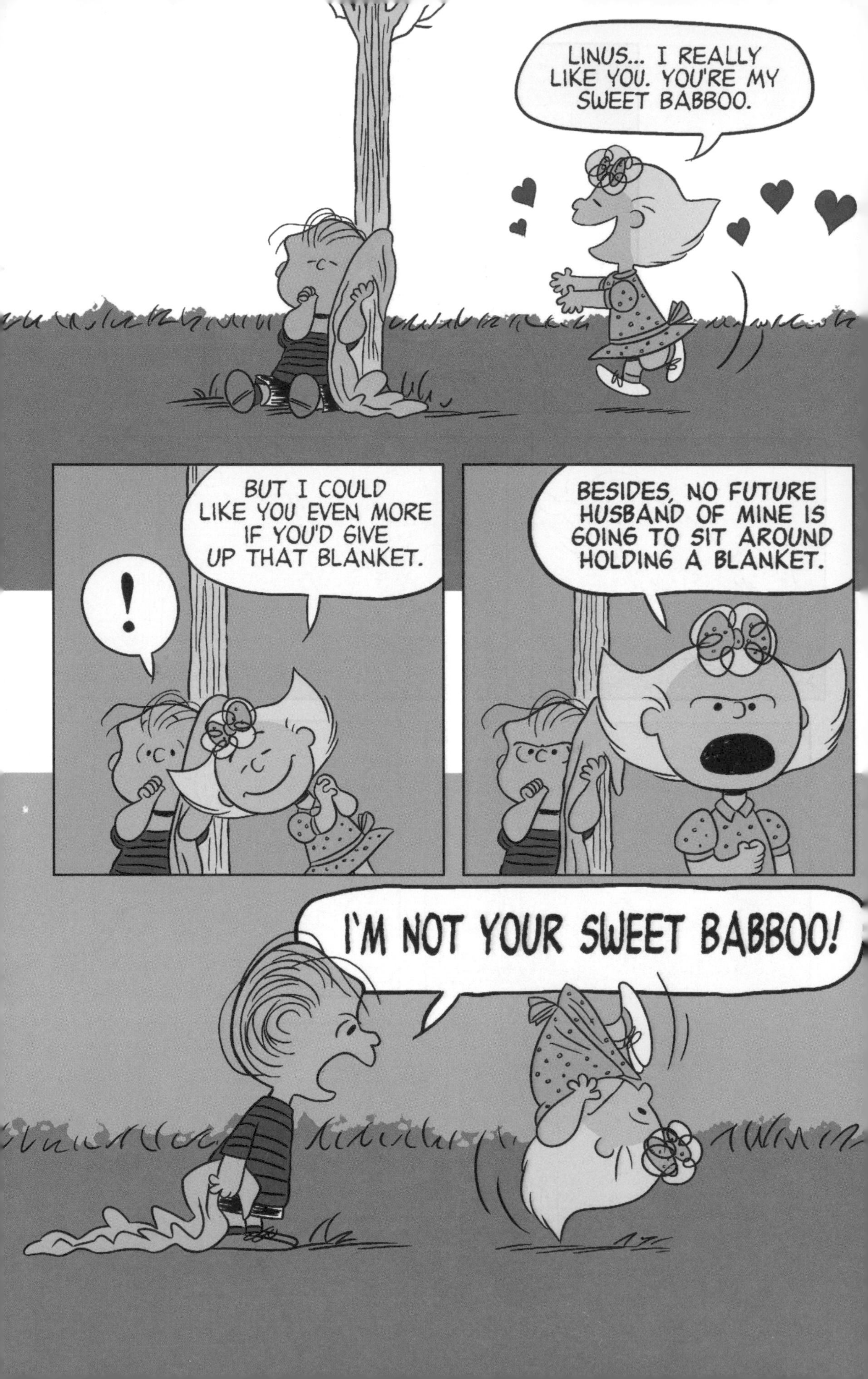
LINUS... I REALLY LIKE YOU. YOU'RE MY SWEET BABBOO.
!
BUT I COULD LIKE YOU EVEN MORE IF YOU'D GIVE UP THAT BLANKET.
BESIDES, NO FUTURE HUSBAND OF MINE IS GOING TO SIT AROUND HOLDING A BLANKET.
I'M NOT YOUR SWEET BABBOO!

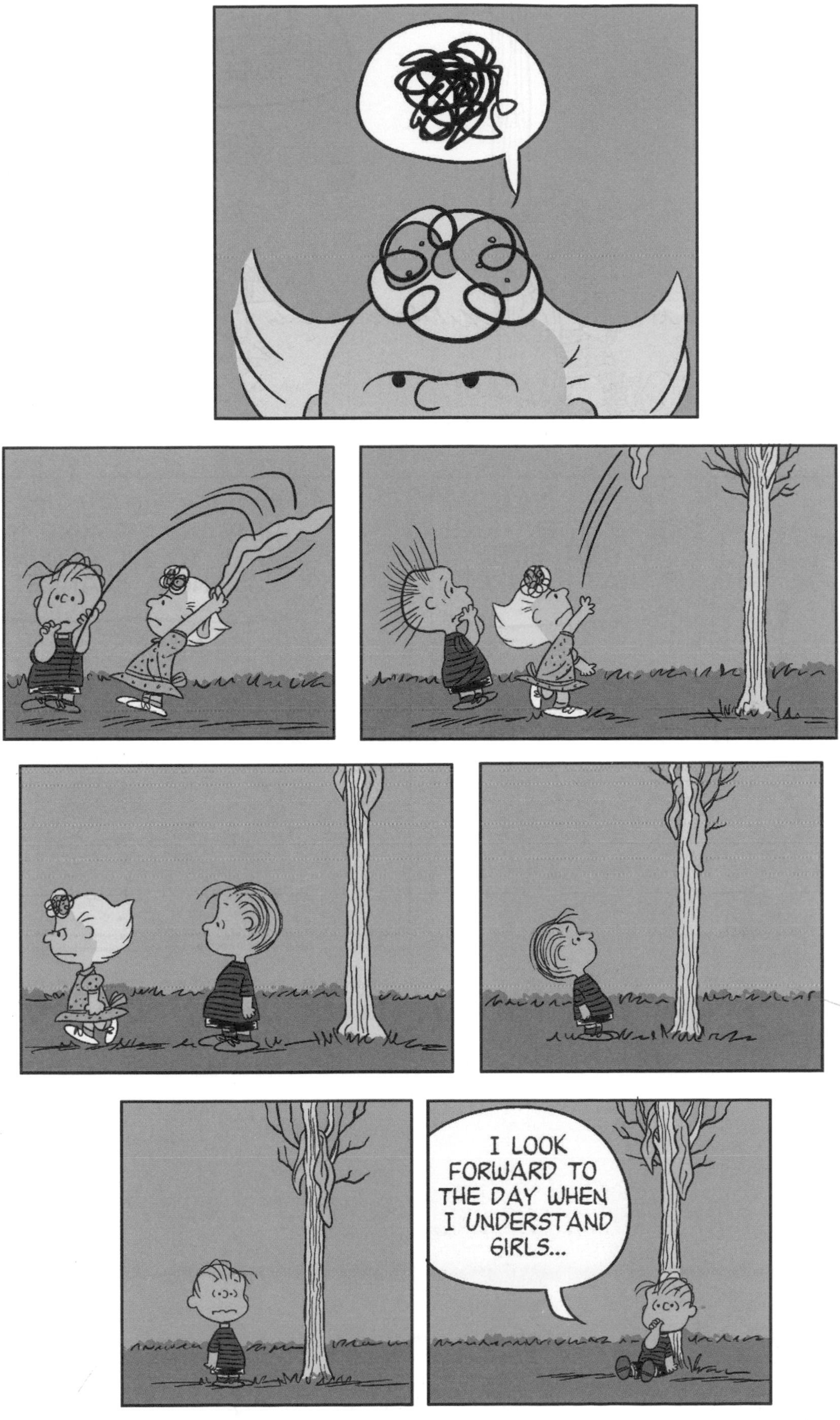
I LOOK FORWARD TO THE DAY WHEN I UNDERSTAND GIRLS...

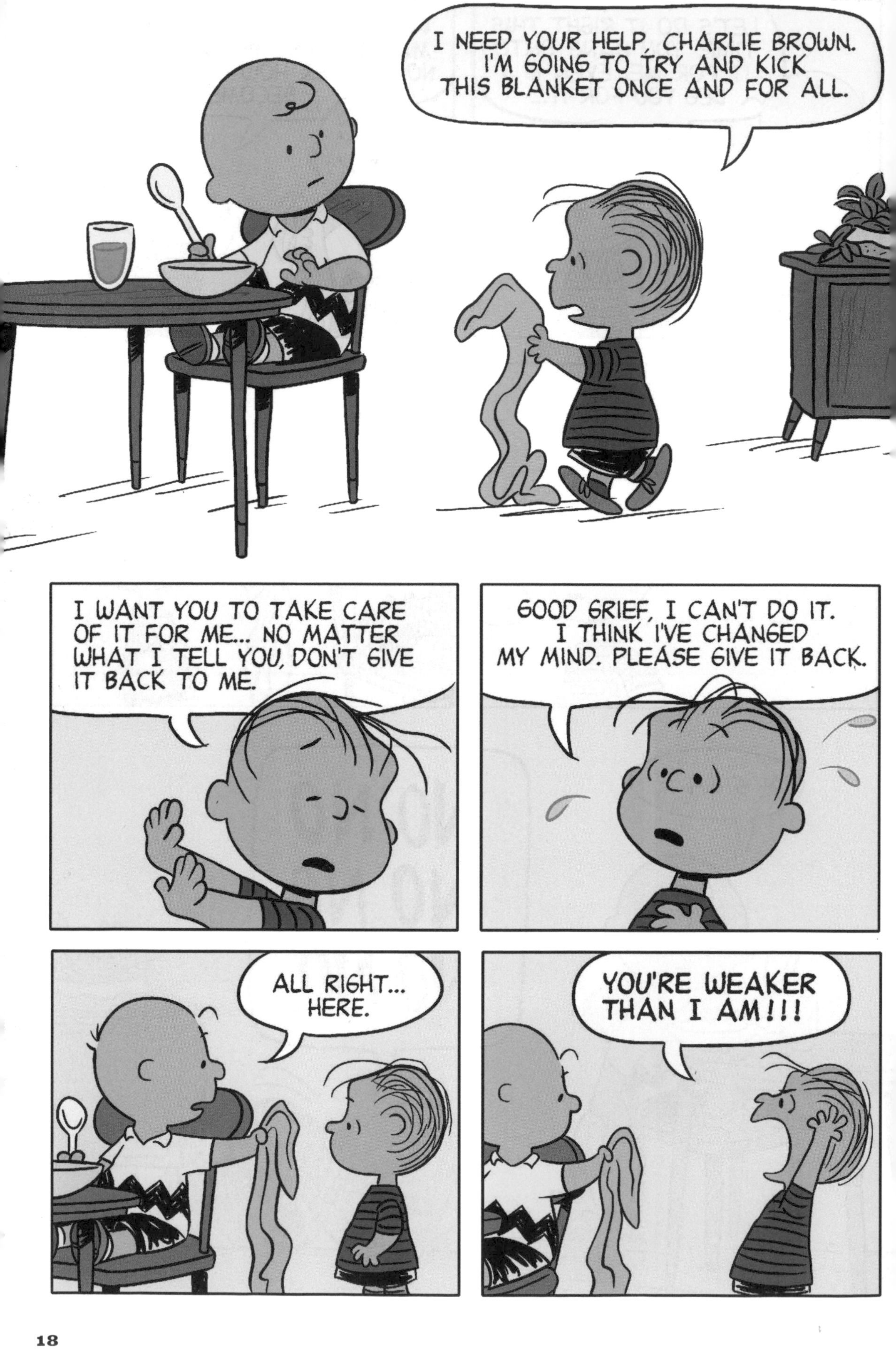
I NEED YOUR HELP, CHARLIE BROWN. I'M GOING TO TRY AND KICK THIS BLANKET ONCE AND FOR ALL.
I WANT YOU TO TAKE CARE OF IT FOR ME... NO MATTER WHAT I TELL YOU, DON'T GIVE IT BACK TO ME.
GOOD GRIEF, I CAN'T DO IT. I THINK I'VE CHANGED MY MIND. PLEASE GIVE IT BACK.
ALL RIGHT... HERE.
YOU'RE WEAKER THAN I AM!!!

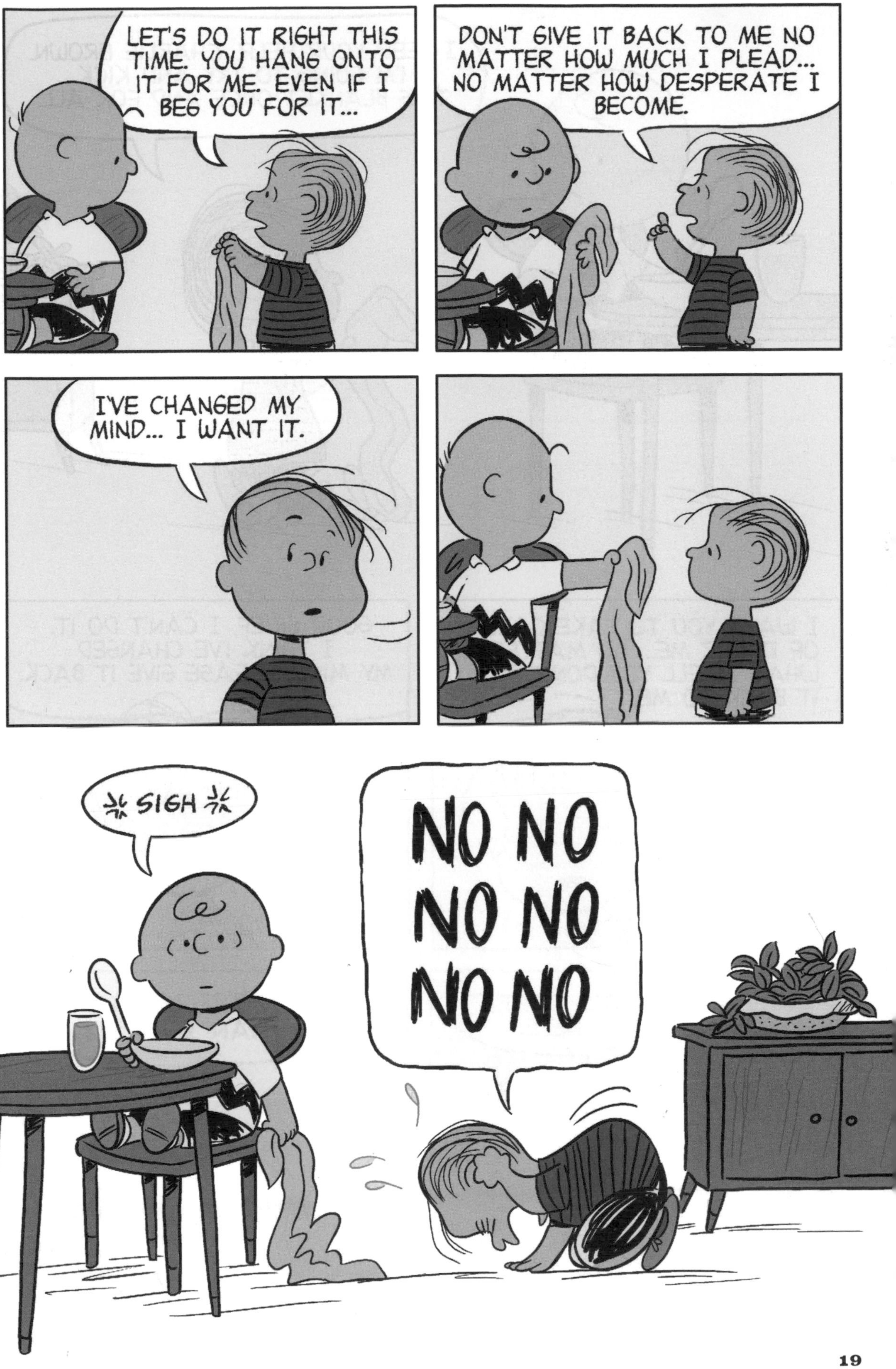
LET'S DO IT RIGHT THIS TIME. YOU HANG ONTO IT FOR ME. EVEN IF I BEG YOU FOR IT...
DON'T GIVE IT BACK TO ME NO MATTER HOW MUCH I PLEAD... NO MATTER HOW DESPERATE I BECOME.
I'VE CHANGED MY MIND... I WANT IT.
SIGH
NO NO NO NO NO NO

WHAT IN THE WORLD ARE YOU DOING HERE?

HE. 5¢

THE DOCTOR IS **IN**

I NEED PROFESSIONAL HELP. I CAN'T GET RID OF THIS BLANKET. I'M IN SAD SHAPE.

WELL, AS THEY SAY ON T.V., THE FACT THAT YOU REALIZE YOU NEED HELP INDICATES THAT YOU ARE NOT TOO FAR GONE.

HAVE NO FEAR, LITTLE BROTHER, MY JOB IS TO BE THAT VOICE GENTLY WHISPERING SOUND ADVICE INTO YOUR EAR.

GROW UP!!!

TOO MUCH HEALING CAN BE DANGEROUS TO YOUR HEALTH.

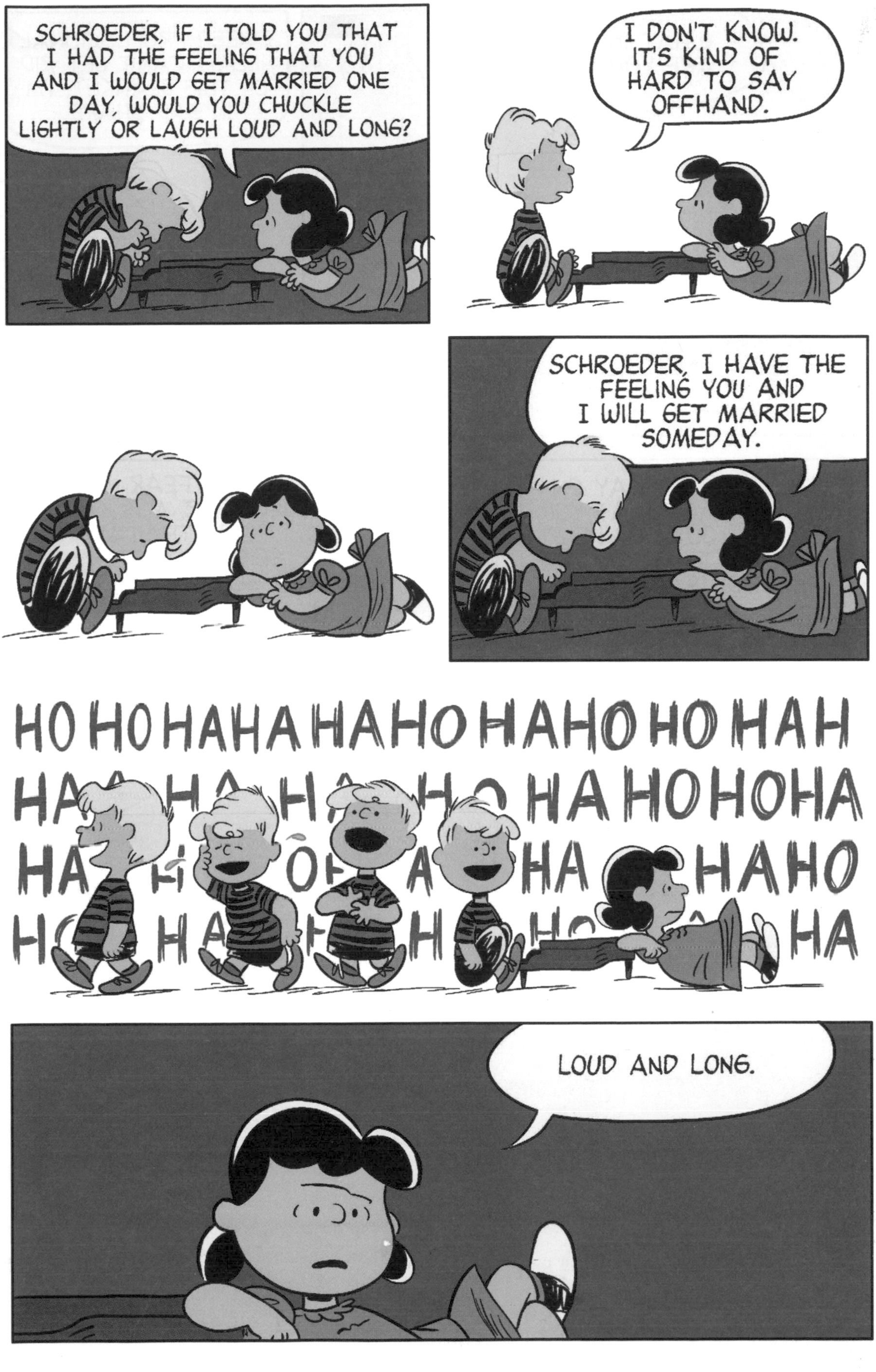
SCHROEDER, IF I TOLD YOU THAT I HAD THE FEELING THAT YOU AND I WOULD GET MARRIED ONE DAY, WOULD YOU CHUCKLE LIGHTLY OR LAUGH LOUD AND LONG?
I DON'T KNOW. IT'S KIND OF HARD TO SAY OFFHAND.
SCHROEDER, I HAVE THE FEELING YOU AND I WILL GET MARRIED SOMEDAY.
HO HO HAHA HAHO HAHO HO HAH
HA HO HO HA
HA HO
HA
LOUD AND LONG.

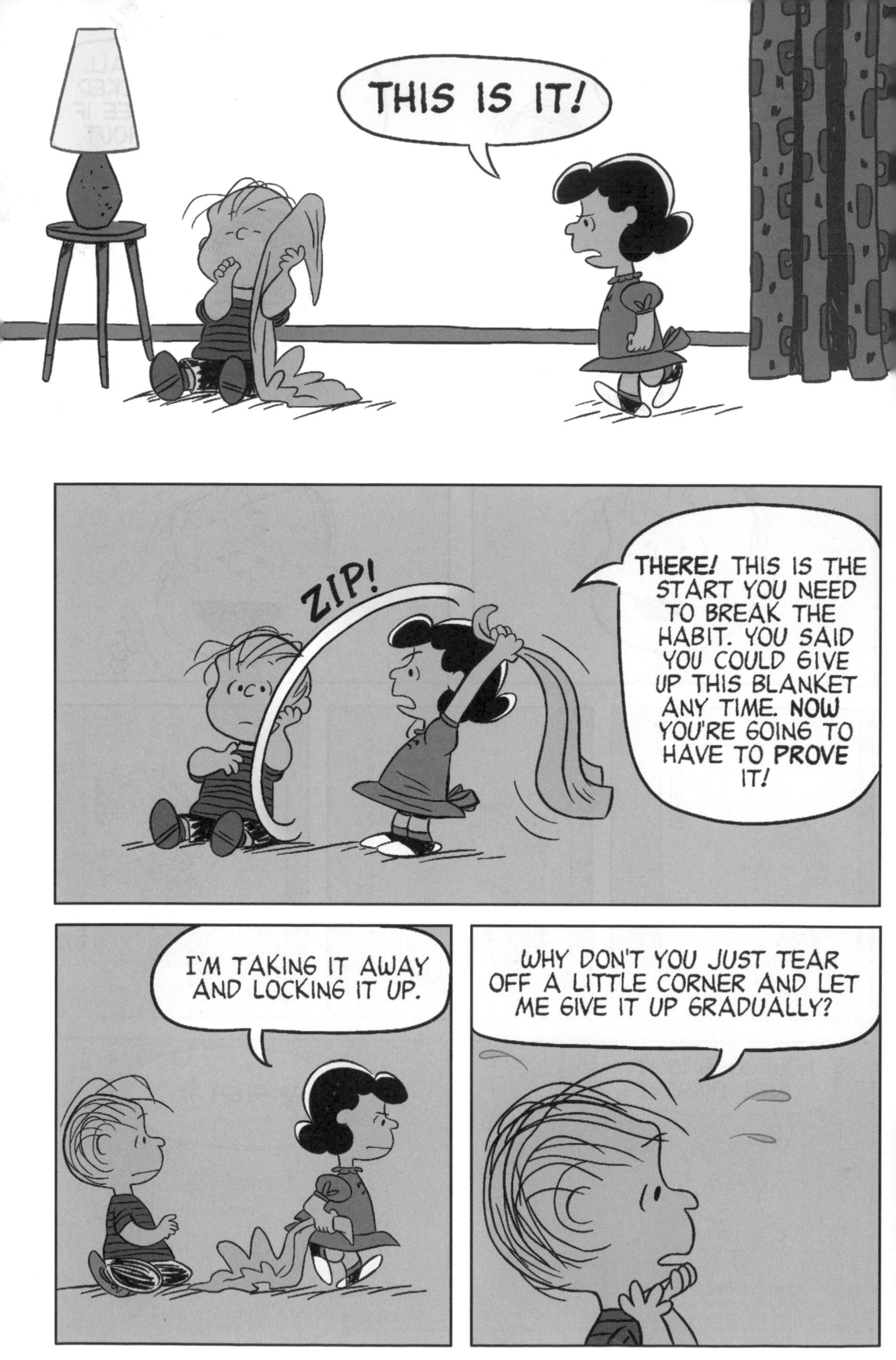
THIS IS IT!
ZIP!
THERE! THIS IS THE START YOU NEED TO BREAK THE HABIT. YOU SAID YOU COULD GIVE UP THIS BLANKET ANY TIME. NOW YOU'RE GOING TO HAVE TO PROVE IT!
I'M TAKING IT AWAY AND LOCKING IT UP.
WHY DON'T YOU JUST TEAR OFF A LITTLE CORNER AND LET ME GIVE IT UP GRADUALLY?

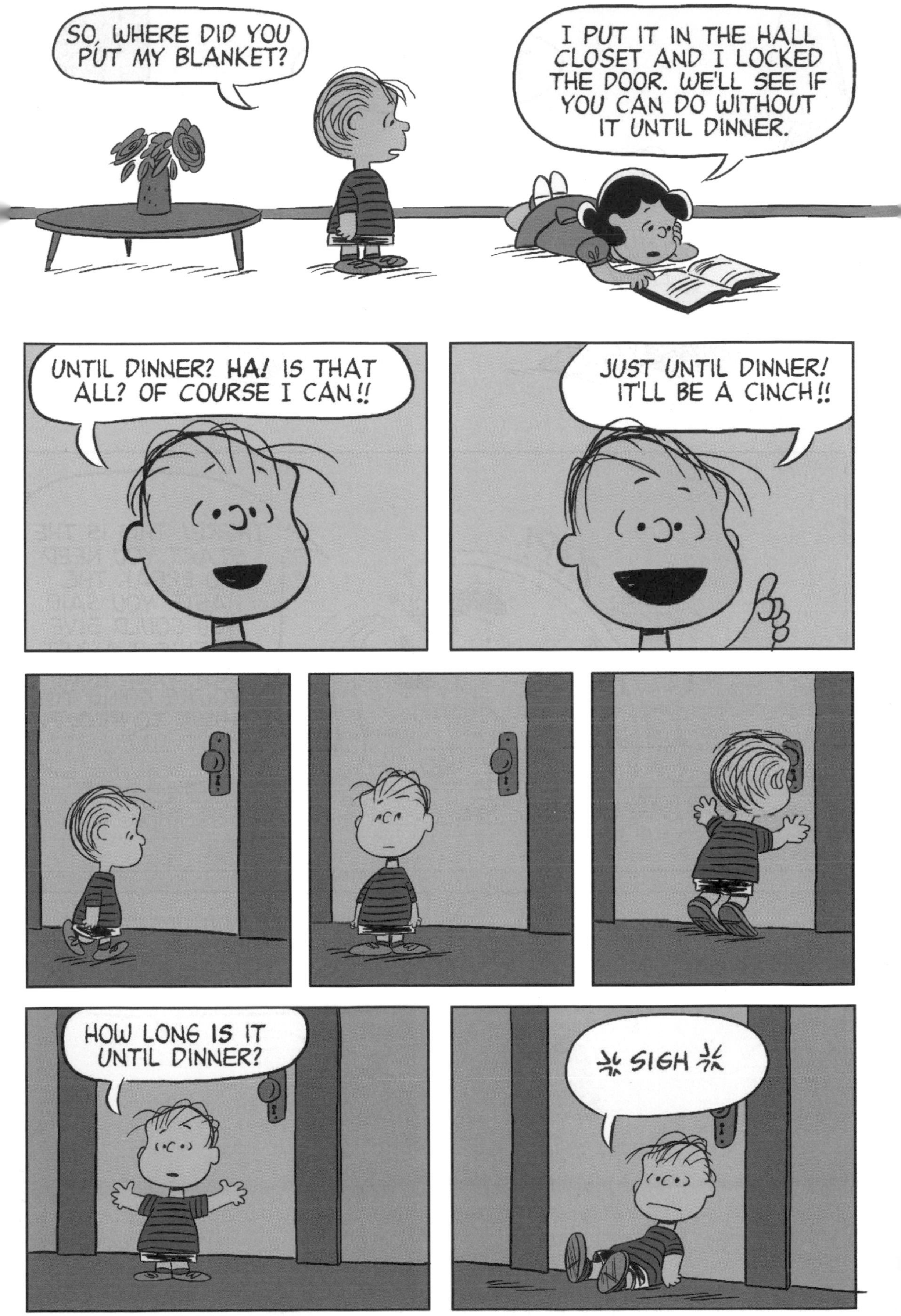
SO, WHERE DID YOU PUT MY BLANKET?
I PUT IT IN THE HALL CLOSET AND I LOCKED THE DOOR. WE'LL SEE IF YOU CAN DO WITHOUT IT UNTIL DINNER.
UNTIL DINNER? HA! IS THAT ALL? OF COURSE I CAN!!
JUST UNTIL DINNER! IT'LL BE A CINCH!!
HOW LONG IS IT UNTIL DINNER?
SIGH

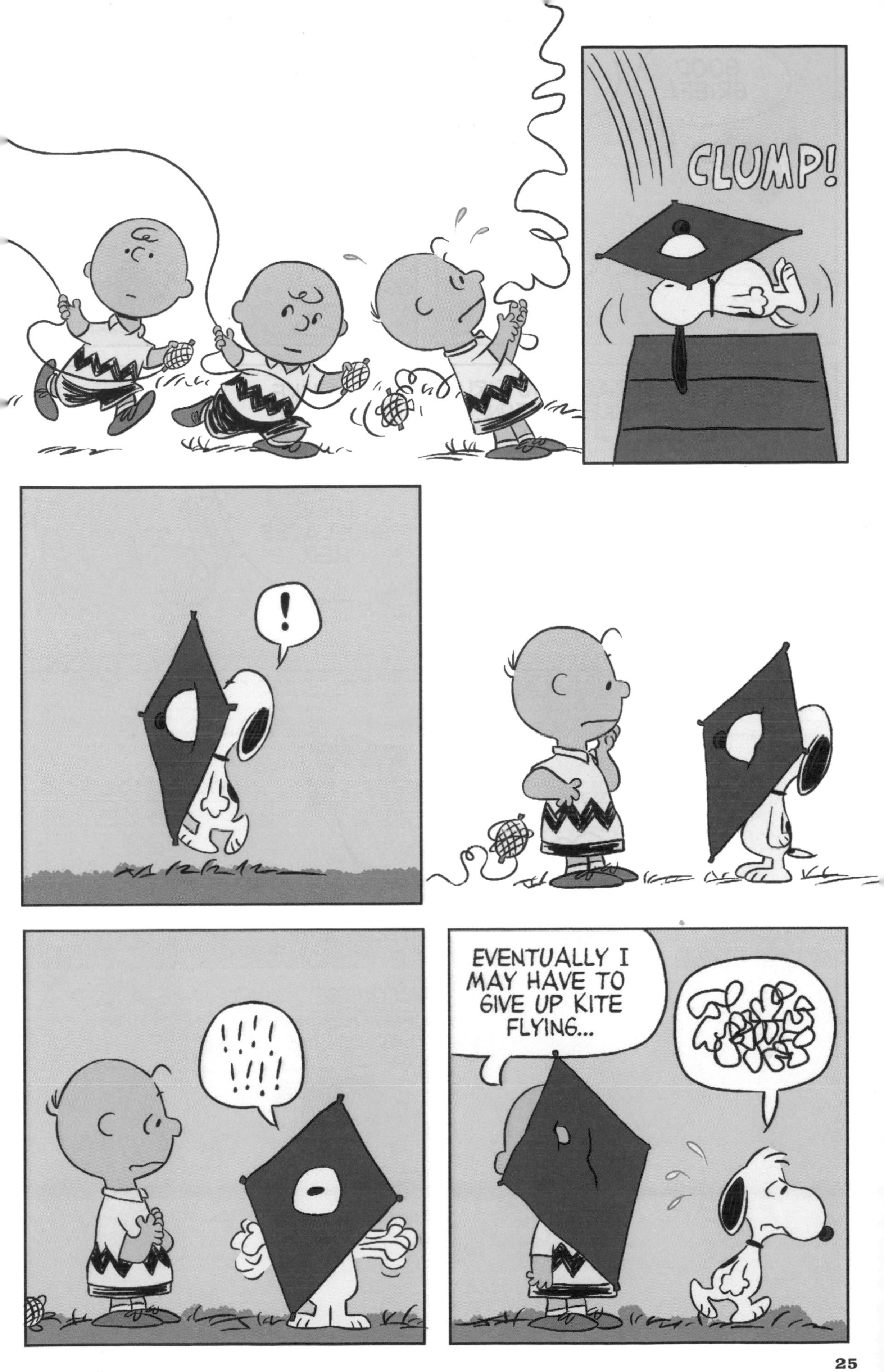
CLUMP!
!
!!!!
!!!!
EVENTUALLY I MAY HAVE TO GIVE UP KITE FLYING...

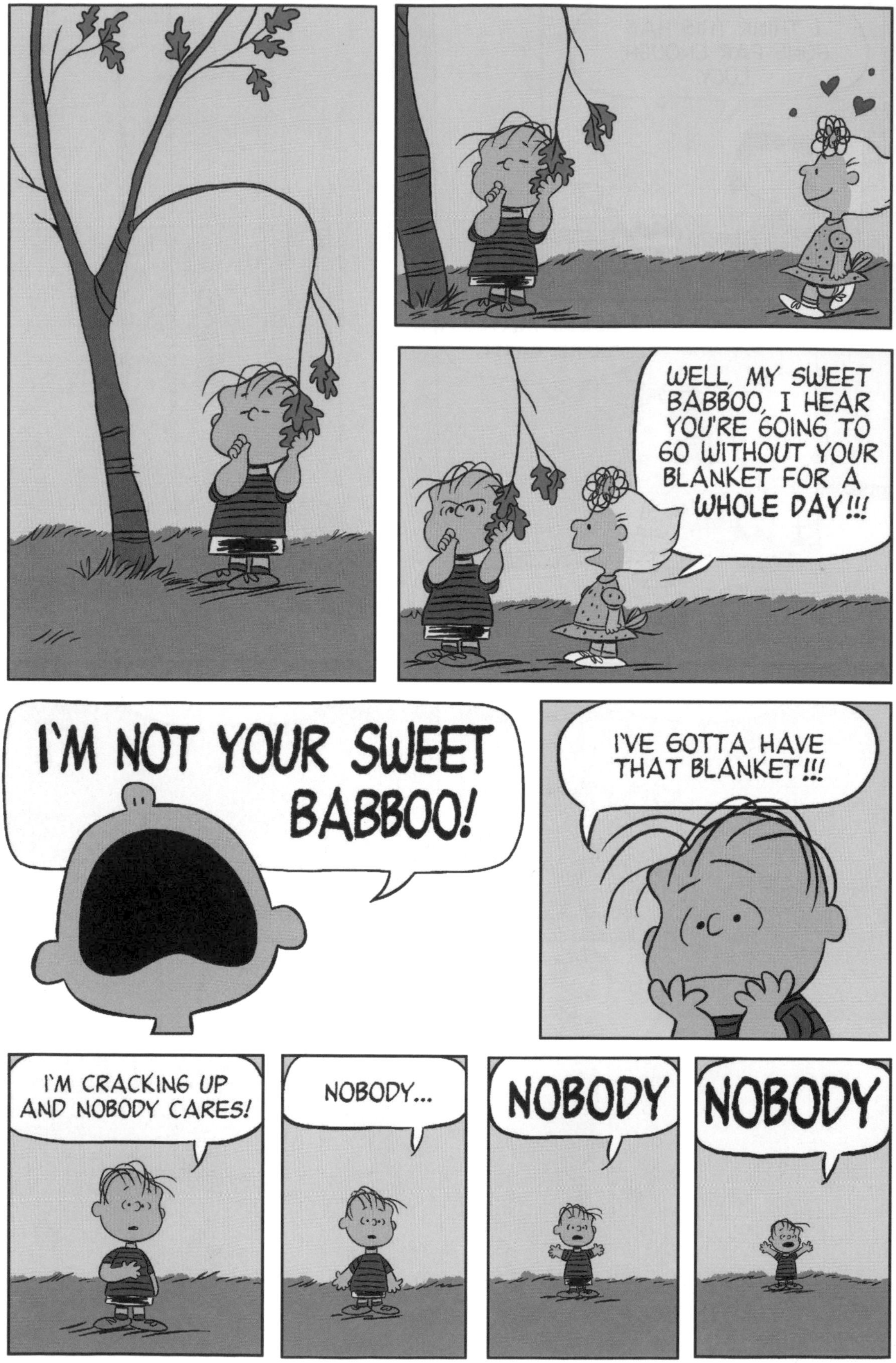
WELL, MY SWEET BABBOO, I HEAR YOU'RE GOING TO GO WITHOUT YOUR BLANKET FOR A WHOLE DAY!!!
I'M NOT YOUR SWEET BABBOO!
I'VE GOTTA HAVE THAT BLANKET!!!
I'M CRACKING UP AND NOBODY CARES!
NOBODY...
NOBODY
NOBODY

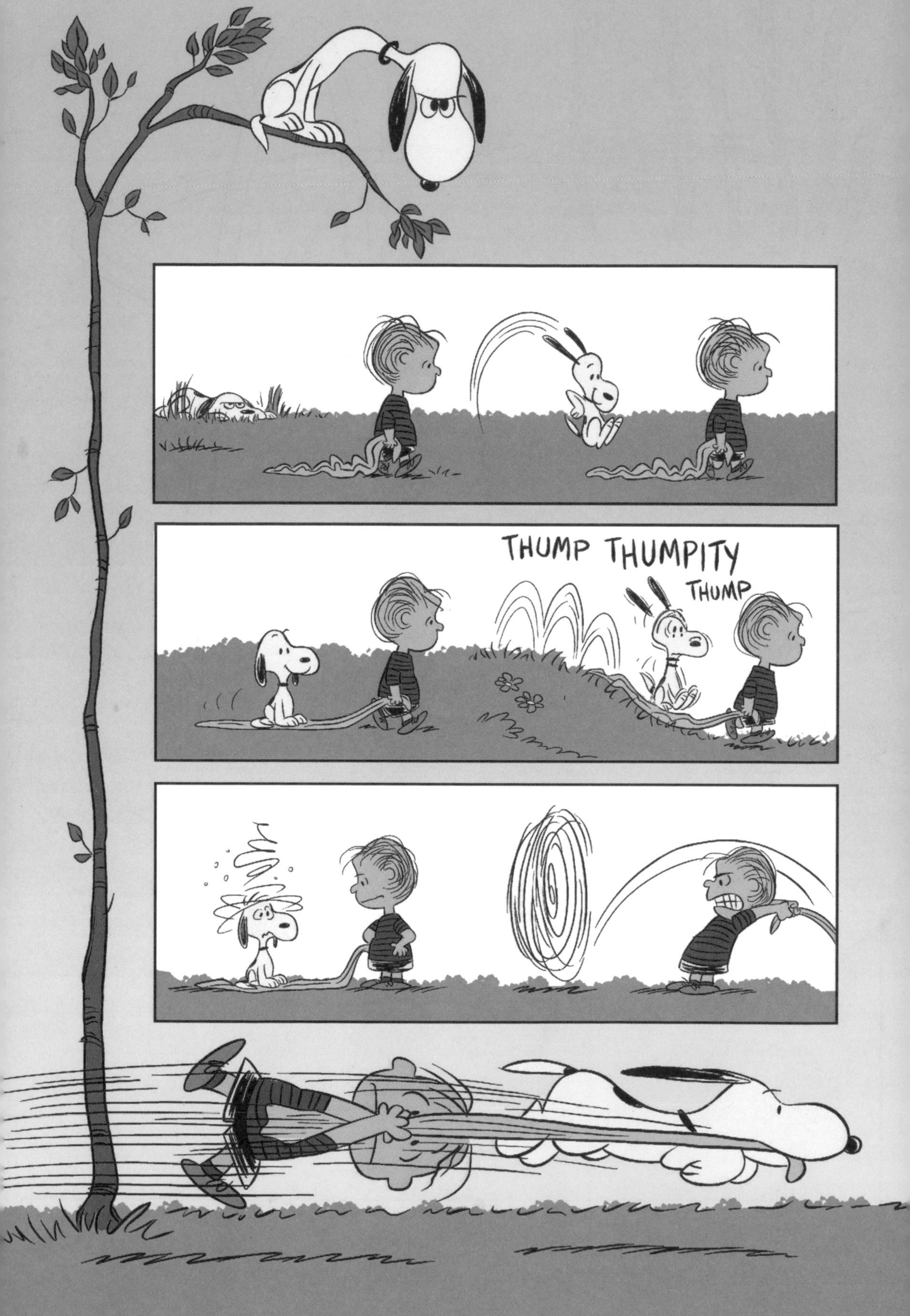
THUMP THUMPITY
THUMP

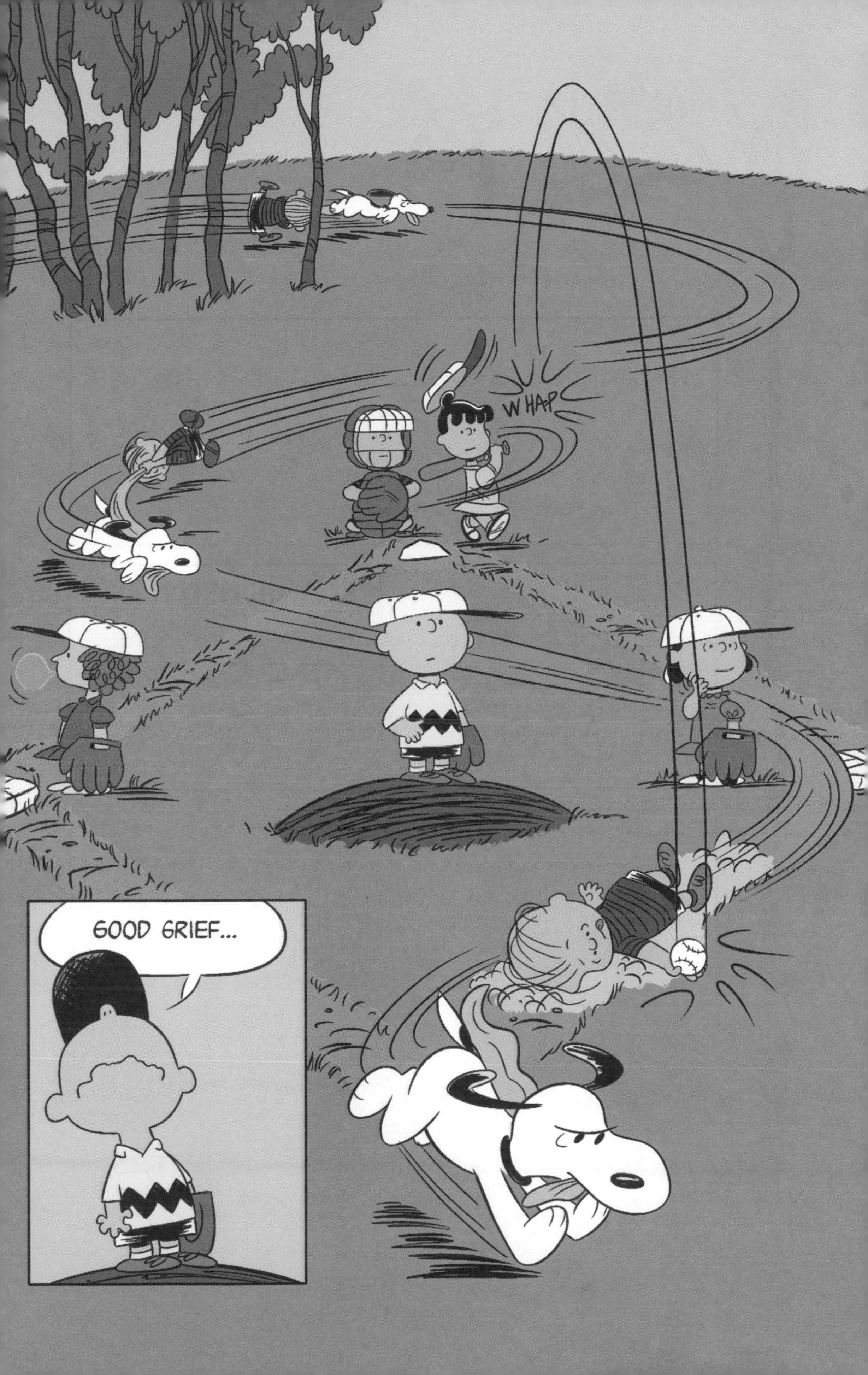
WHAP
GOOD GRIEF...

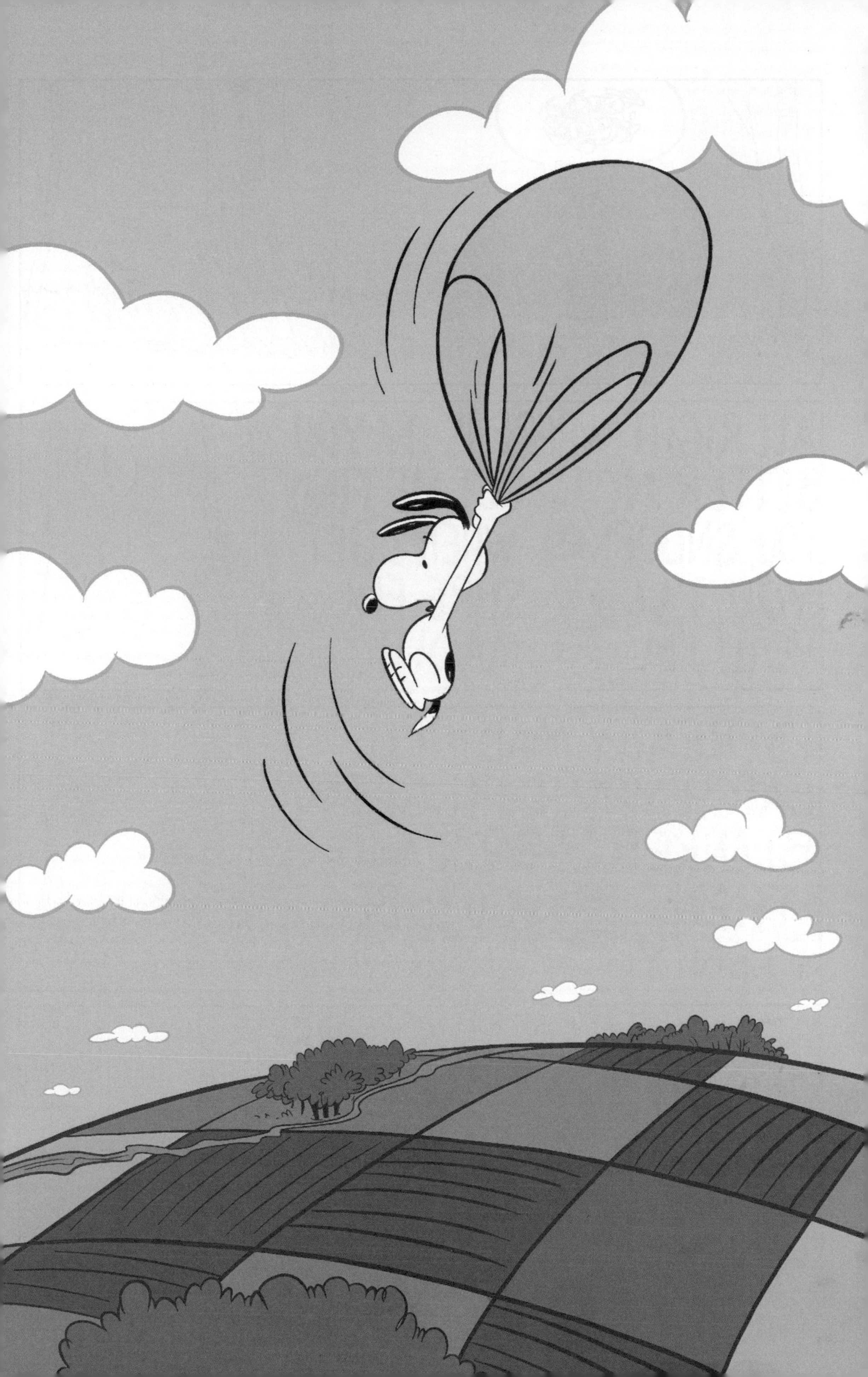

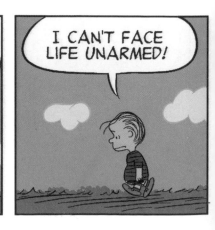

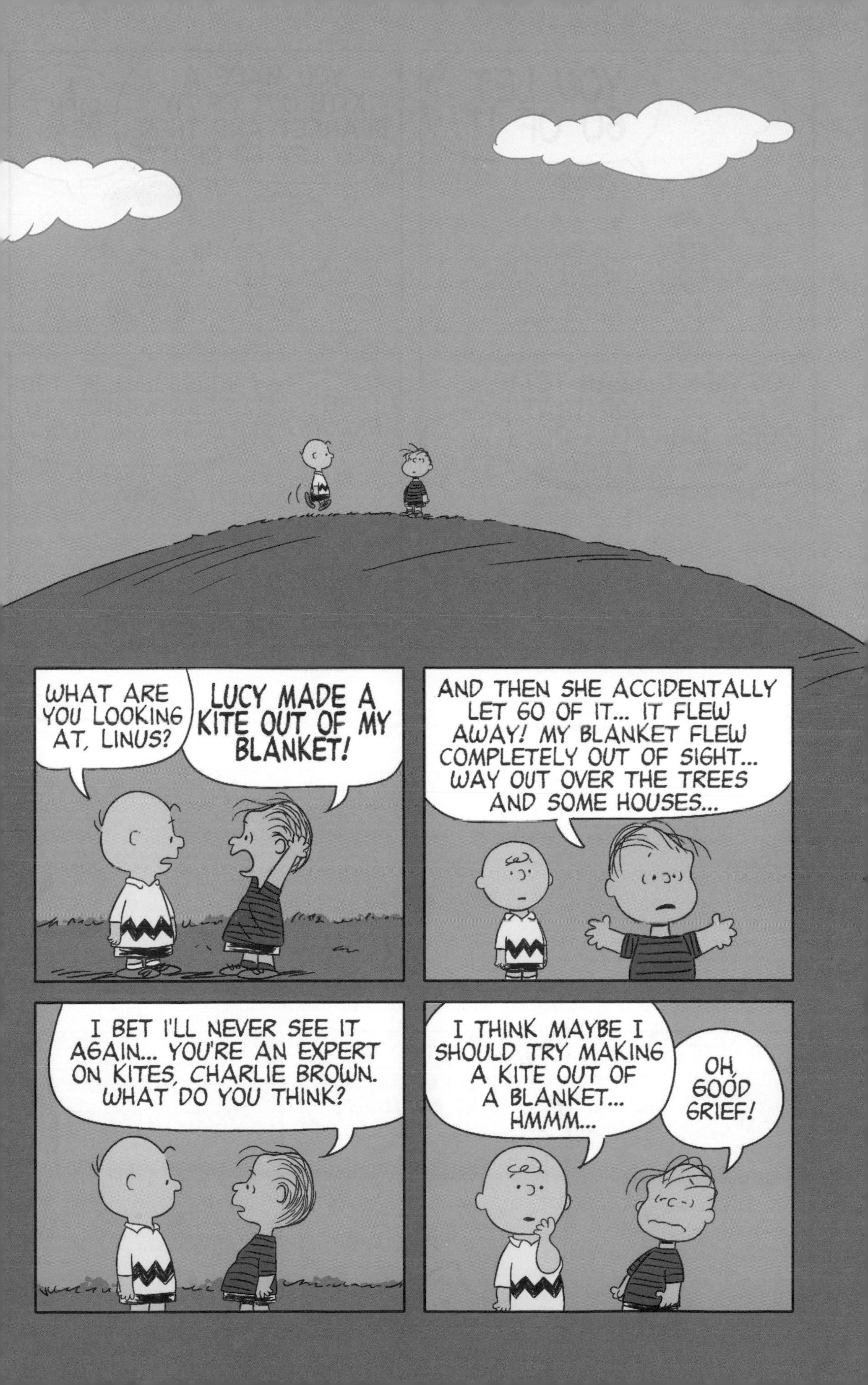
WHAT ARE YOU LOOKING AT, LINUS?
LUCY MADE A KITE OUT OF MY BLANKET!
AND THEN SHE ACCIDENTALLY LET GO OF IT... IT FLEW AWAY! MY BLANKET FLEW COMPLETELY OUT OF SIGHT... WAY OUT OVER THE TREES AND SOME HOUSES...
I BET I'LL NEVER SEE IT AGAIN... YOU'RE AN EXPERT ON KITES, CHARLIE BROWN. WHAT DO YOU THINK?
I THINK MAYBE I SHOULD TRY MAKING A KITE OUT OF A BLANKET... HMMM...
OH, GOOD GRIEF!

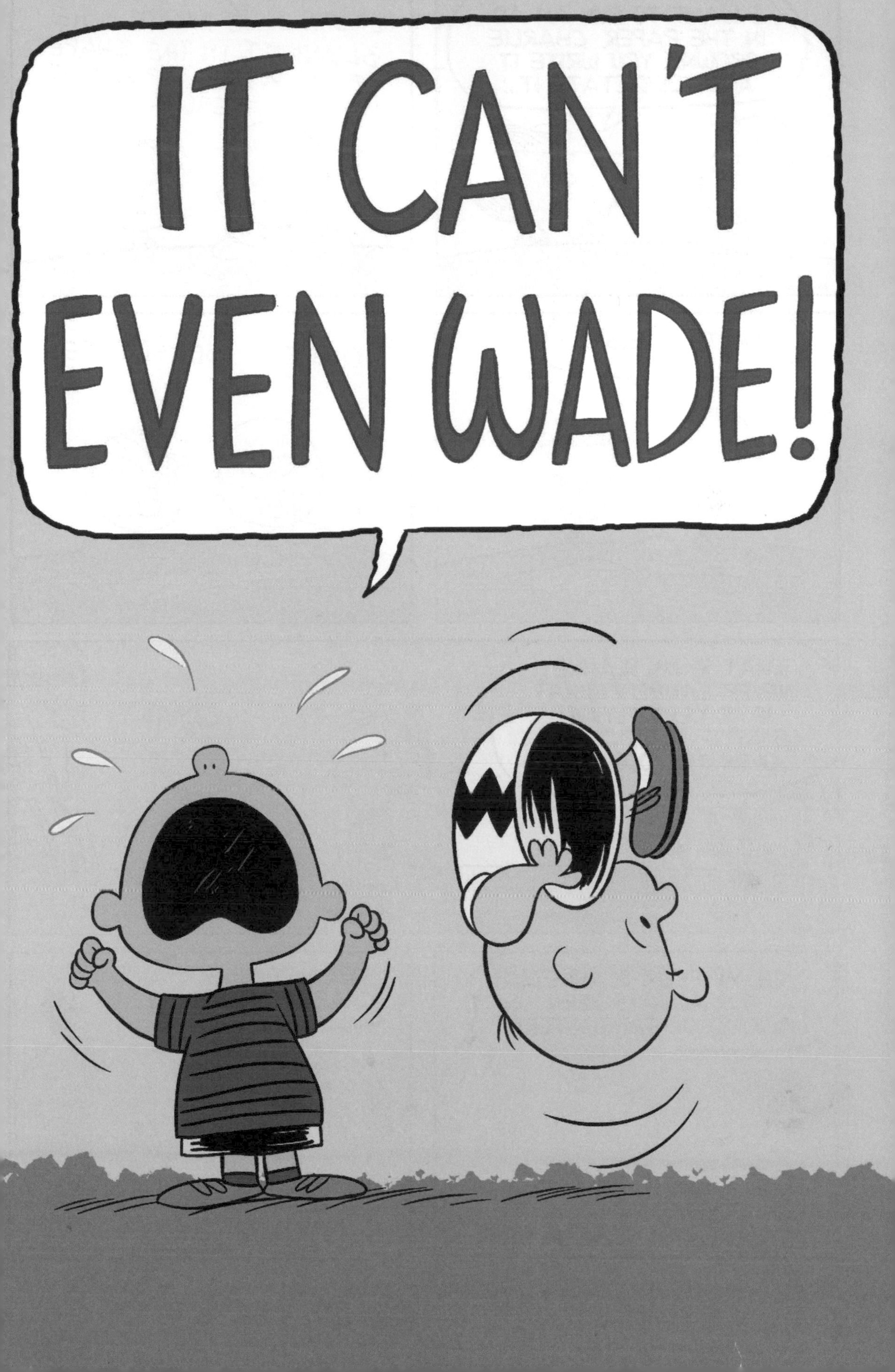
IT CAN'T EVEN WADE!

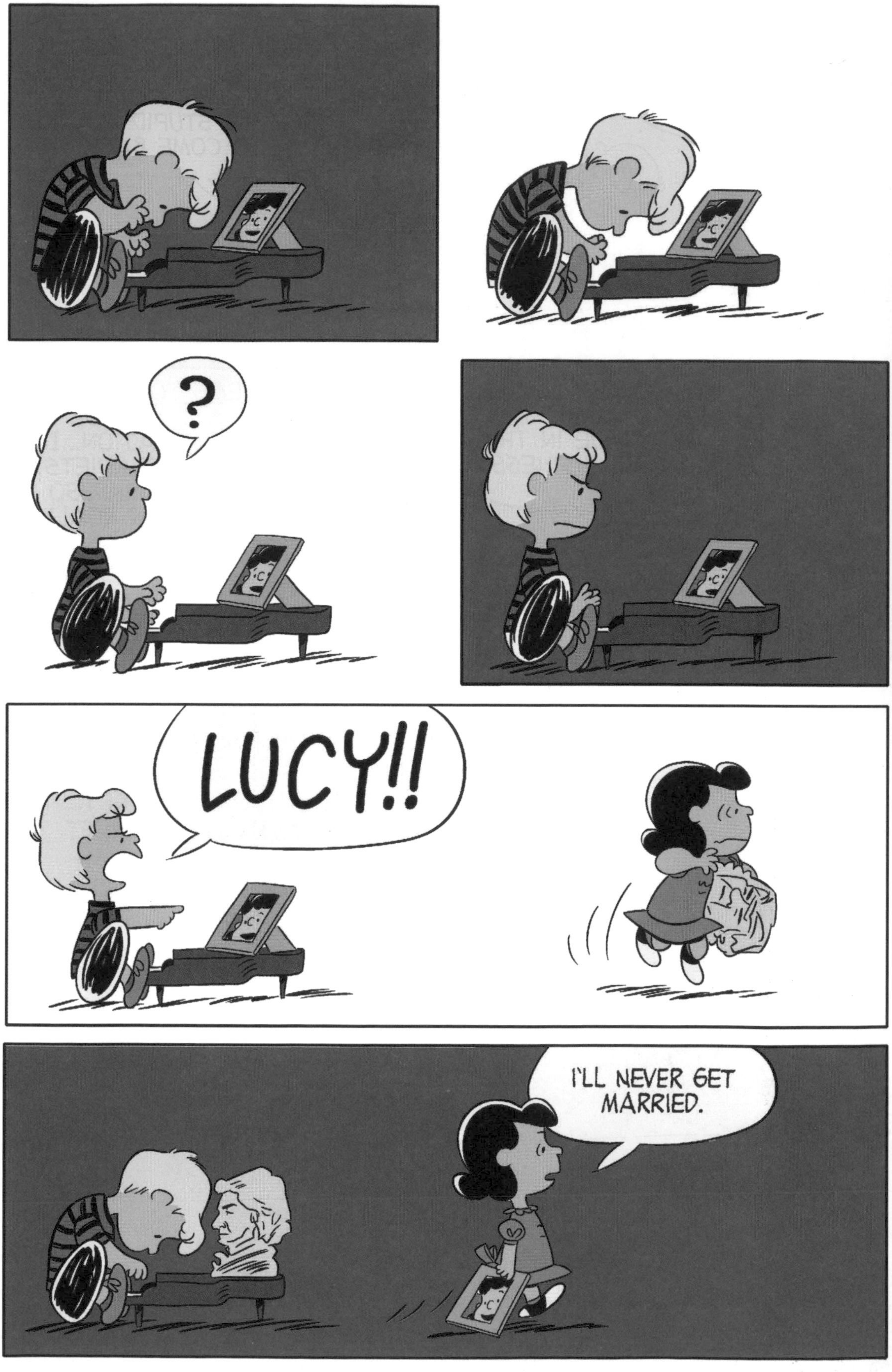
?
LUCY!!
I'LL NEVER GET MARRIED.

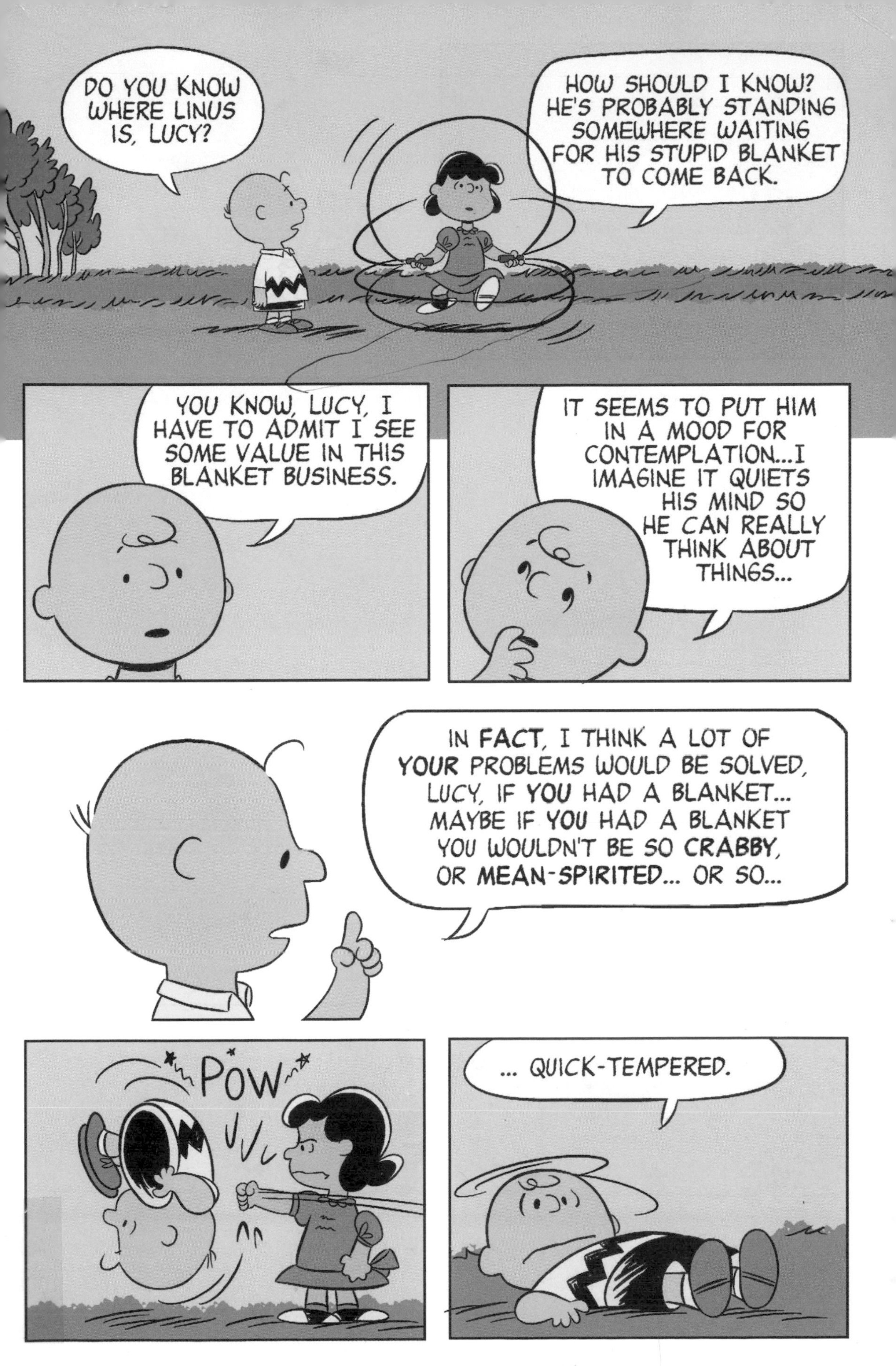
DO YOU KNOW WHERE LINUS IS, LUCY?
HOW SHOULD I KNOW? HE'S PROBABLY STANDING SOMEWHERE WAITING FOR HIS STUPID BLANKET TO COME BACK.
YOU KNOW, LUCY, I HAVE TO ADMIT I SEE SOME VALUE IN THIS BLANKET BUSINESS.
IT SEEMS TO PUT HIM IN A MOOD FOR CONTEMPLATION...I IMAGINE IT QUIETS HIS MIND SO HE CAN REALLY THINK ABOUT THINGS...
IN FACT, I THINK A LOT OF YOUR PROBLEMS WOULD BE SOLVED, LUCY, IF YOU HAD A BLANKET... MAYBE IF YOU HAD A BLANKET YOU WOULDN'T BE SO CRABBY, OR MEAN-SPIRITED... OR SO...
POW
... QUICK-TEMPERED.

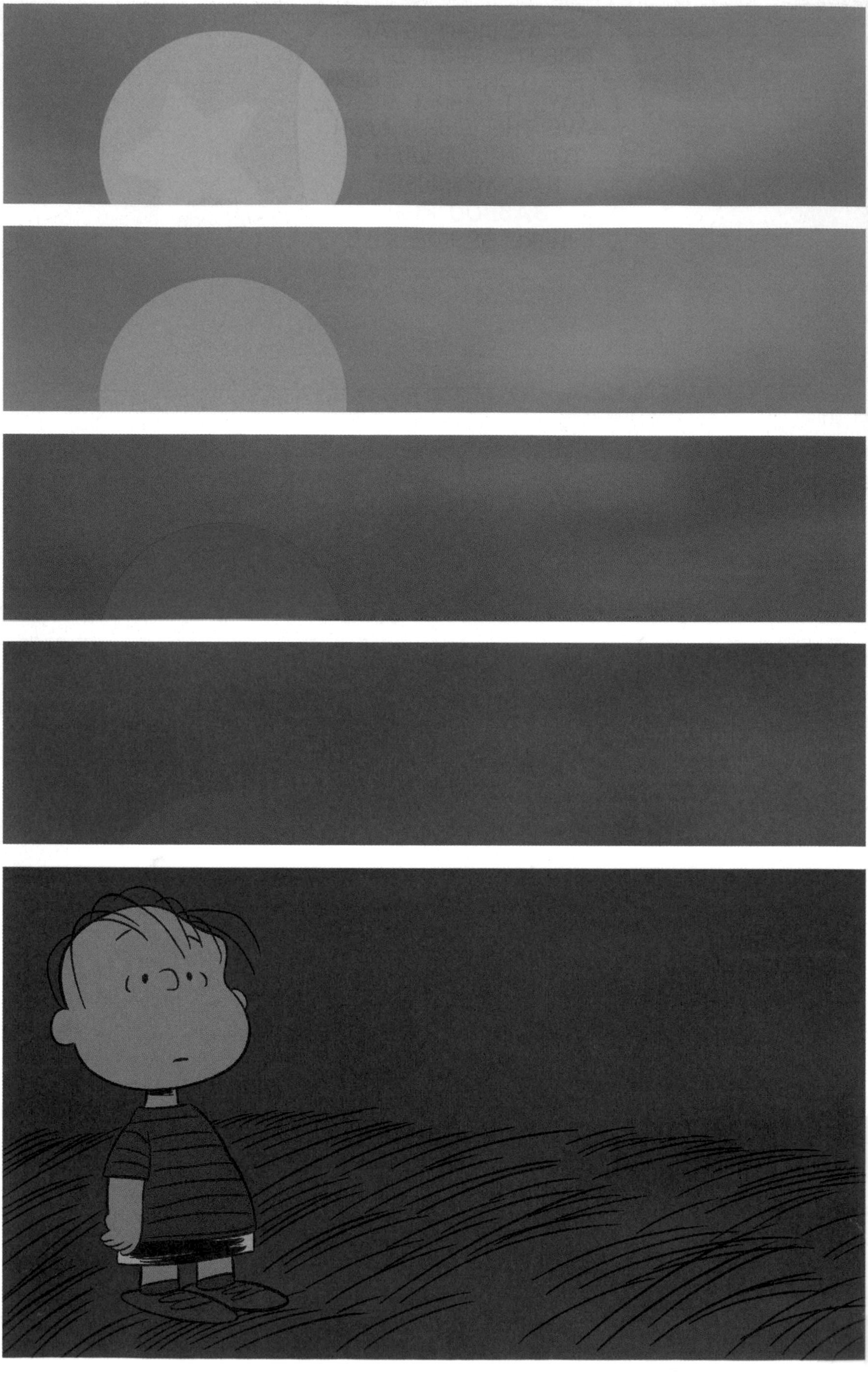

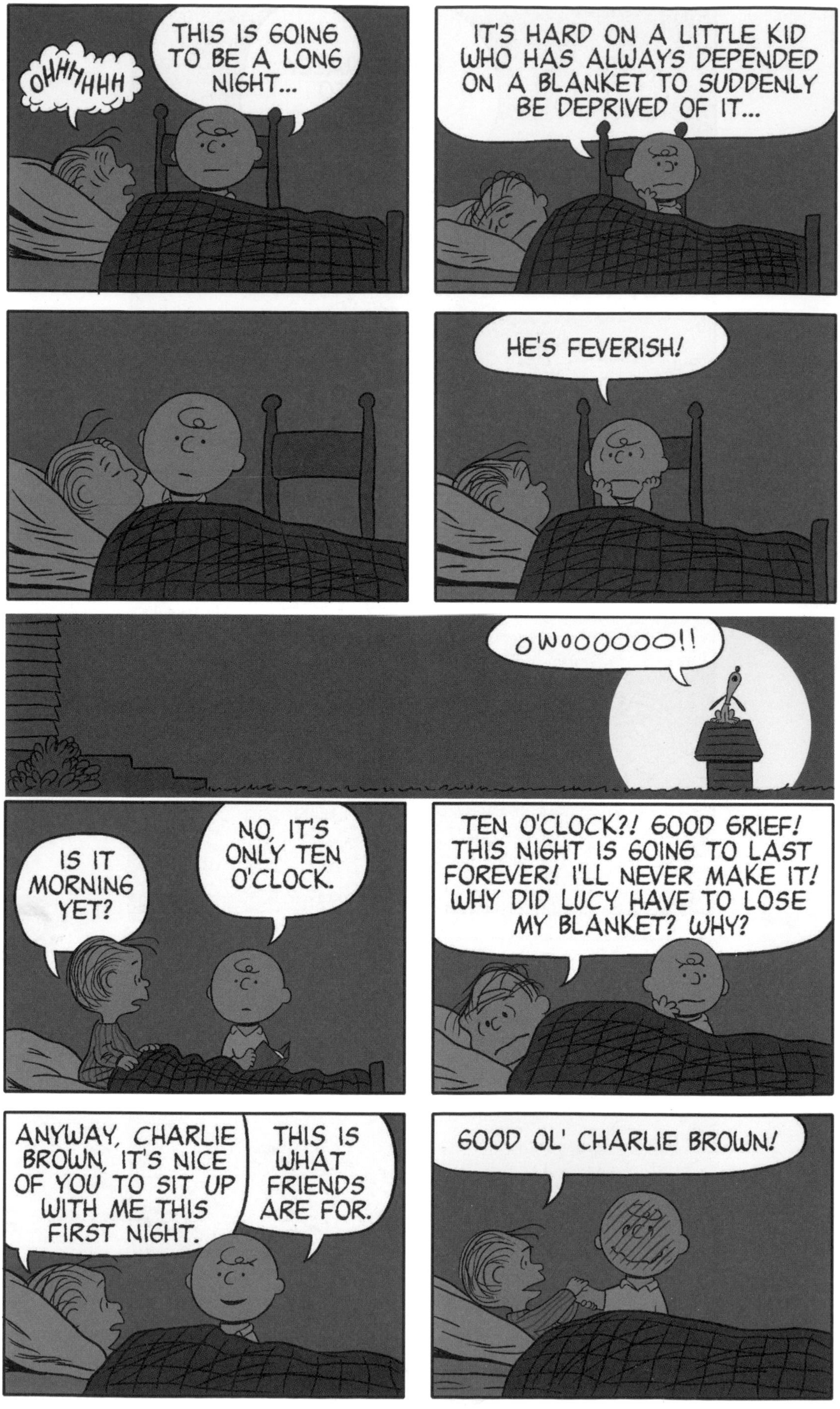
OHHHHHH
THIS IS GOING TO BE A LONG NIGHT...
IT'S HARD ON A LITTLE KID WHO HAS ALWAYS DEPENDED ON A BLANKET TO SUDDENLY BE DEPRIVED OF IT...
HE'S FEVERISH!
OWOOOOOO!!
IS IT MORNING YET?
NO, IT'S ONLY TEN O'CLOCK.
TEN O'CLOCK?! GOOD GRIEF! THIS NIGHT IS GOING TO LAST FOREVER! I'LL NEVER MAKE IT! WHY DID LUCY HAVE TO LOSE MY BLANKET? WHY?
ANYWAY, CHARLIE BROWN, IT'S NICE OF YOU TO SIT UP WITH ME THIS FIRST NIGHT.
THIS IS WHAT FRIENDS ARE FOR.
GOOD OL' CHARLIE BROWN!

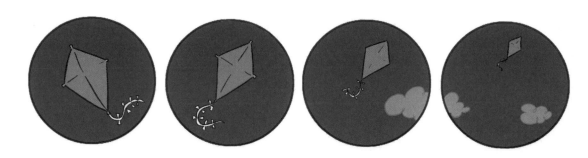

BAM
BAM
BAM

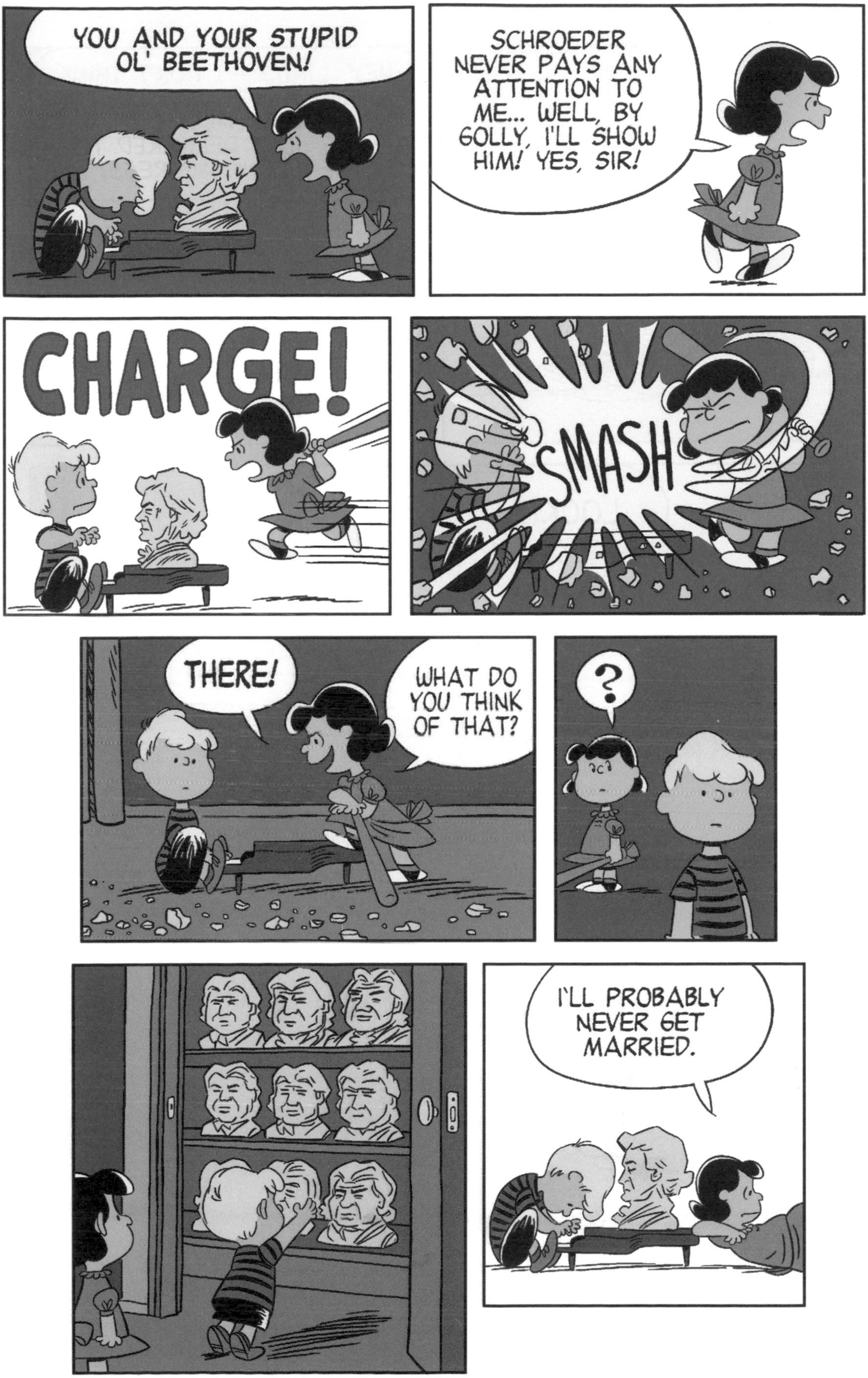
YOU AND YOUR STUPID OL' BEETHOVEN!
SCHROEDER NEVER PAYS ANY ATTENTION TO ME... WELL, BY GOLLY, I'LL SHOW HIM! YES, SIR!
CHARGE!
SMASH
THERE!
WHAT DO YOU THINK OF THAT?
?
I'LL PROBABLY NEVER GET MARRIED.

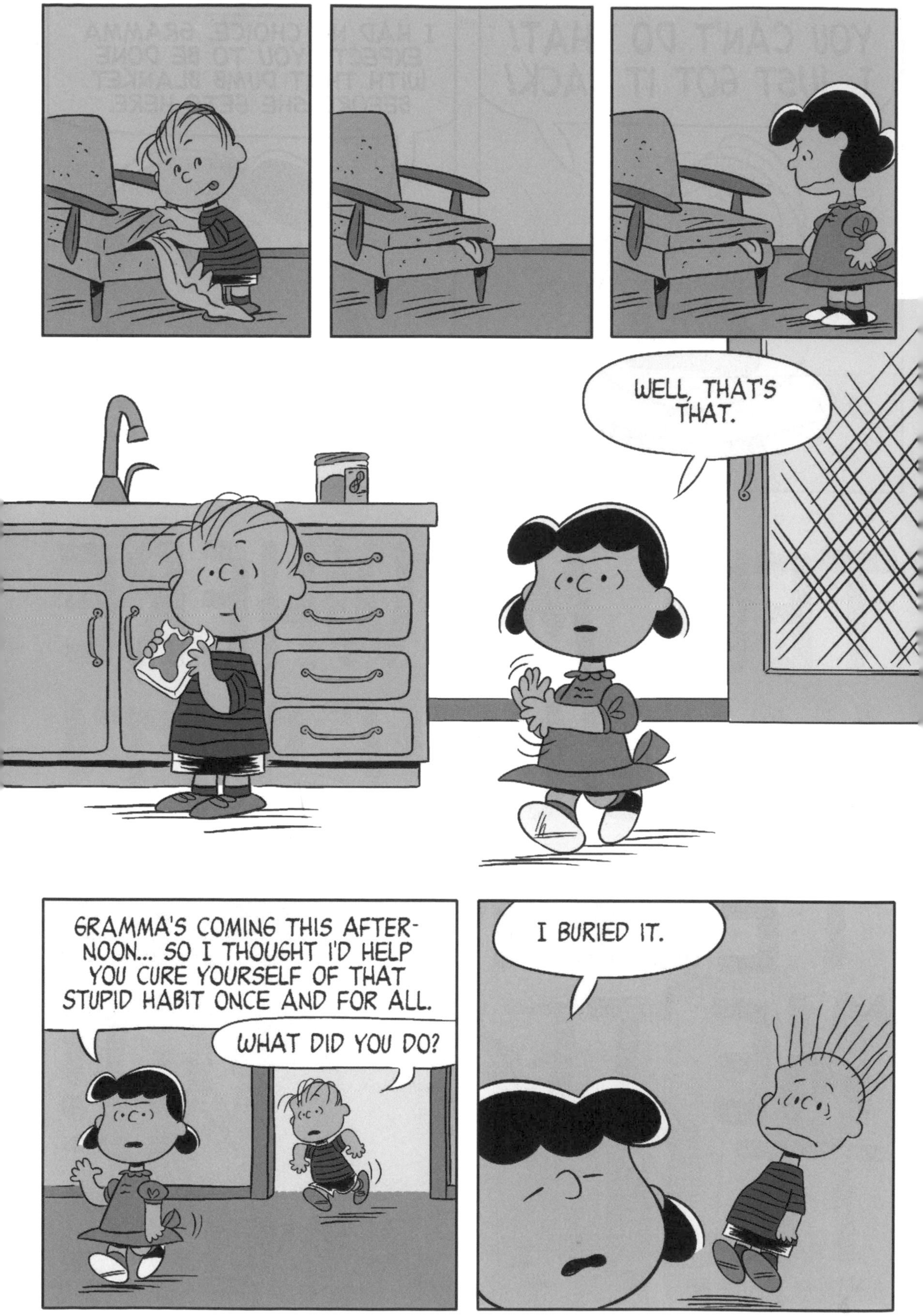
WELL, THAT'S THAT.
GRAMMA'S COMING THIS AFTER-NOON... SO I THOUGHT I'D HELP YOU CURE YOURSELF OF THAT STUPID HABIT ONCE AND FOR ALL.
WHAT DID YOU DO?
I BURIED IT.

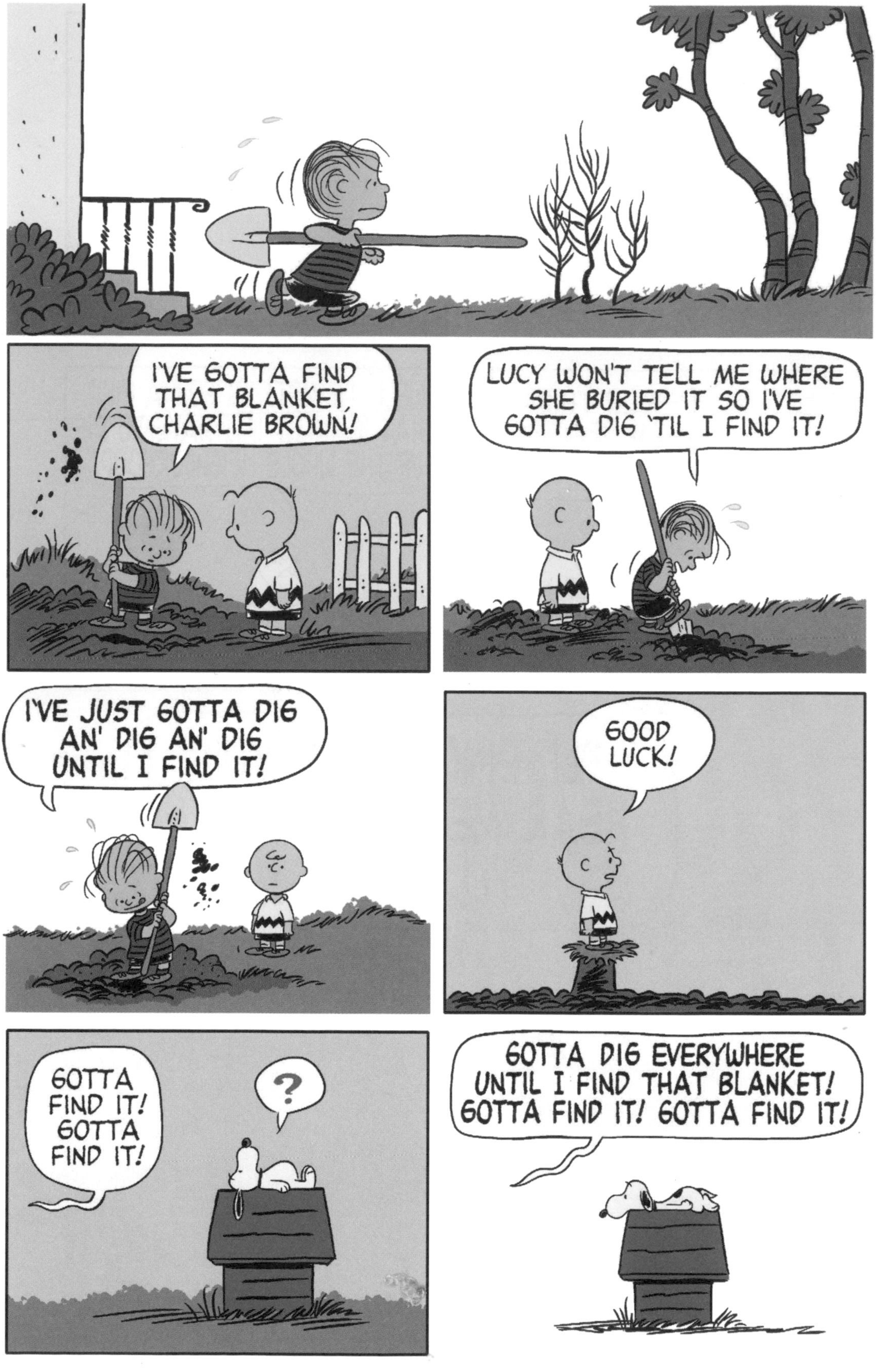
I'VE GOTTA FIND THAT BLANKET, CHARLIE BROWN!
LUCY WON'T TELL ME WHERE SHE BURIED IT SO I'VE GOTTA DIG 'TIL I FIND IT!
I'VE JUST GOTTA DIG AN' DIG AN' DIG UNTIL I FIND IT!
GOOD LUCK!
GOTTA FIND IT! GOTTA FIND IT!
?
GOTTA DIG EVERYWHERE UNTIL I FIND THAT BLANKET! GOTTA FIND IT! GOTTA FIND IT!

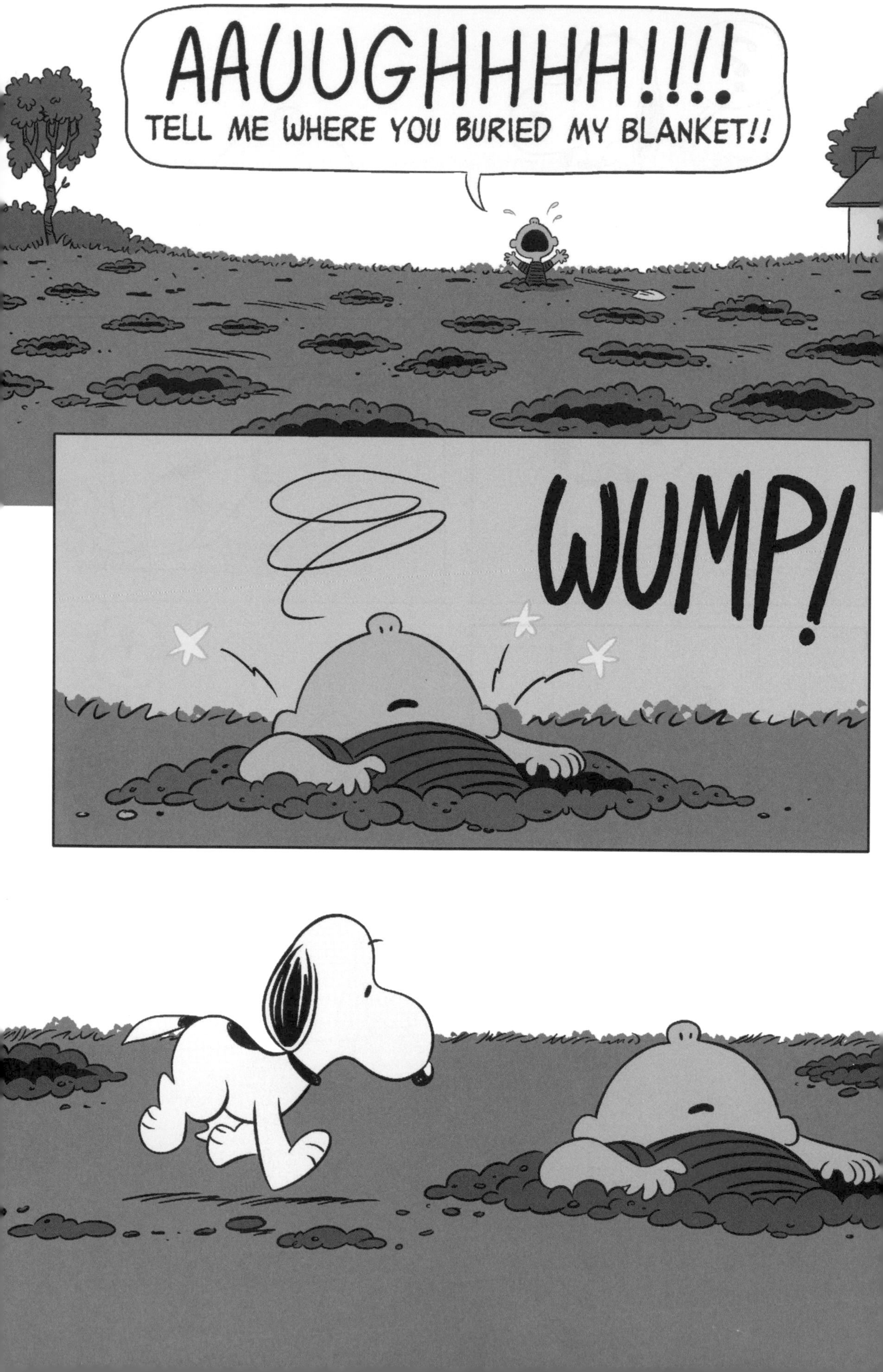
AAUUGHHHH!!!!
TELL ME WHERE YOU BURIED MY BLANKET!!
WUMP!

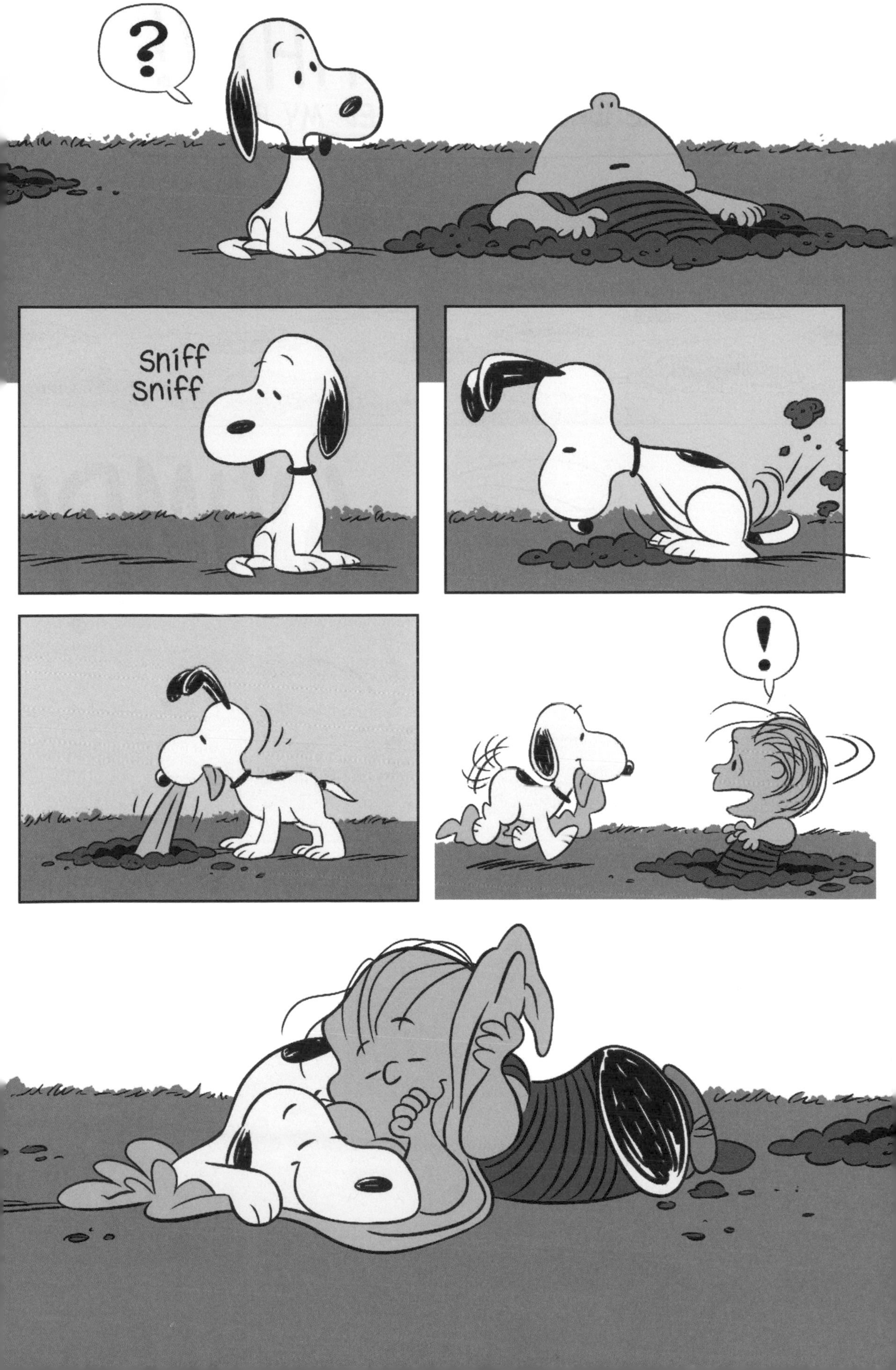
?
Sniff
sniff
!

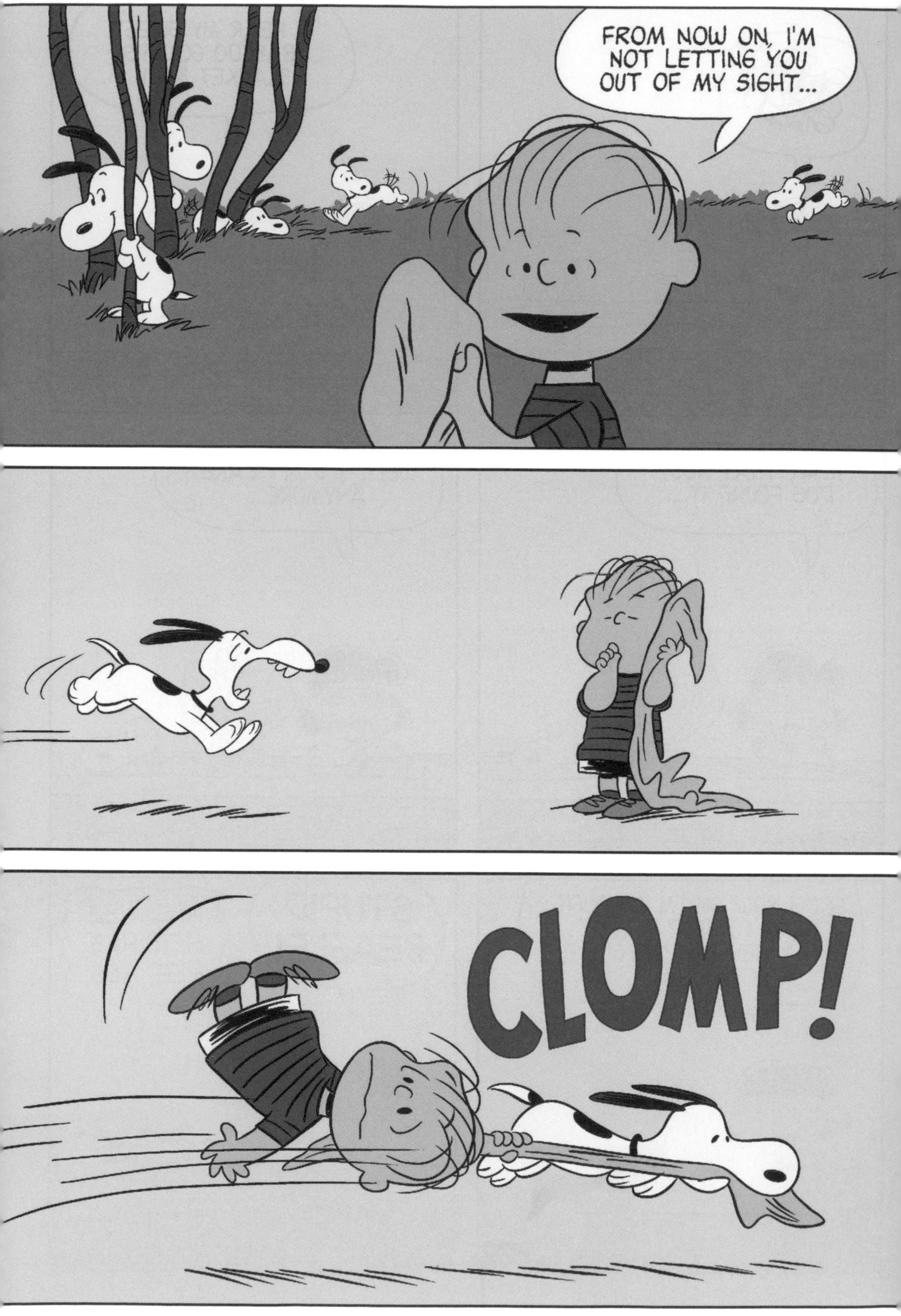
FROM NOW ON, I'M NOT LETTING YOU OUT OF MY SIGHT...
CLOMP!

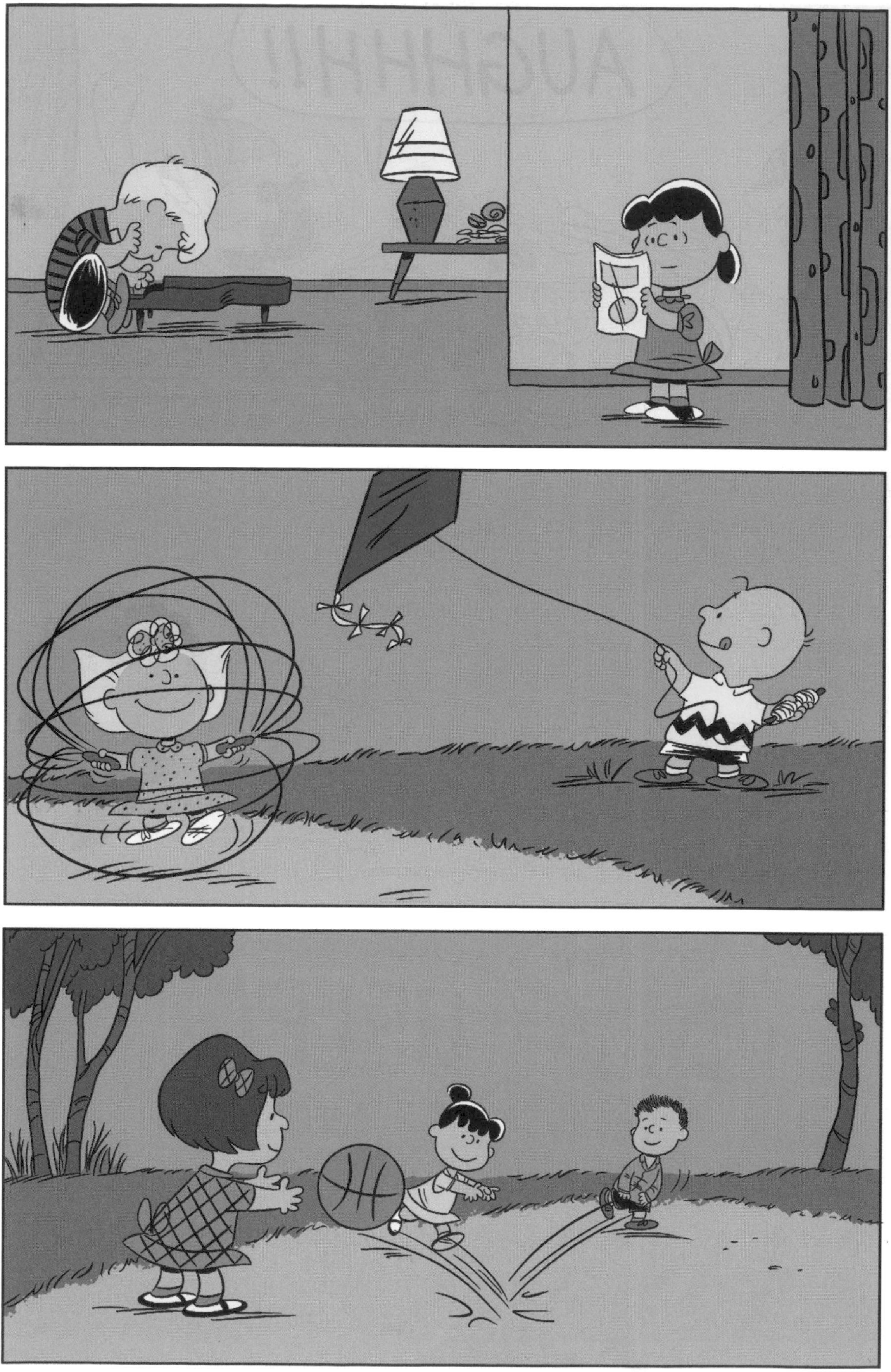

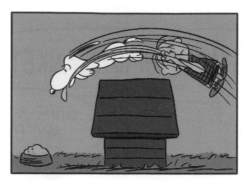

THERE HE IS!!!

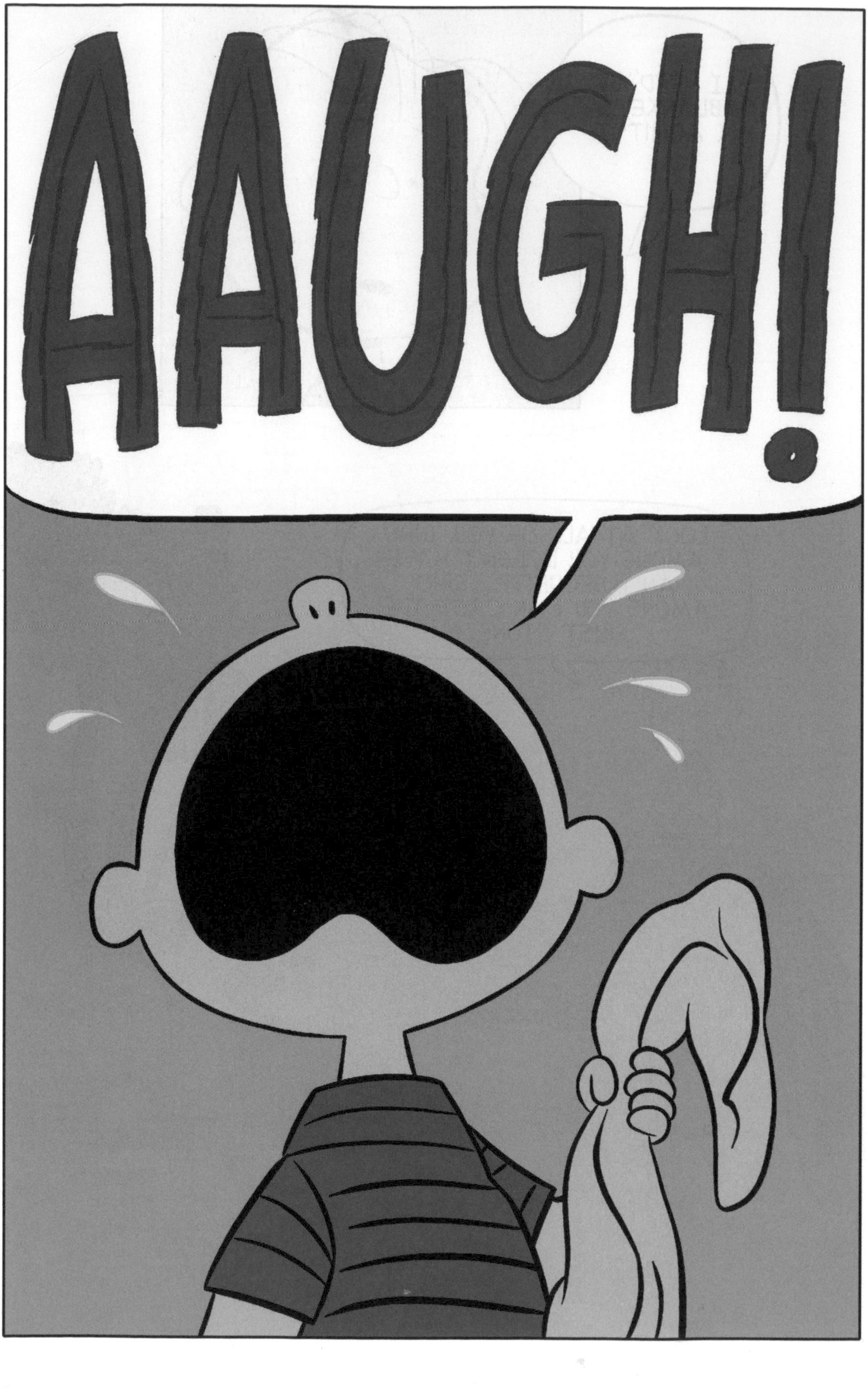
AAUGH!

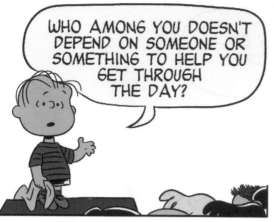

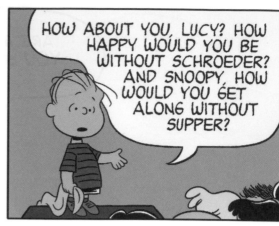

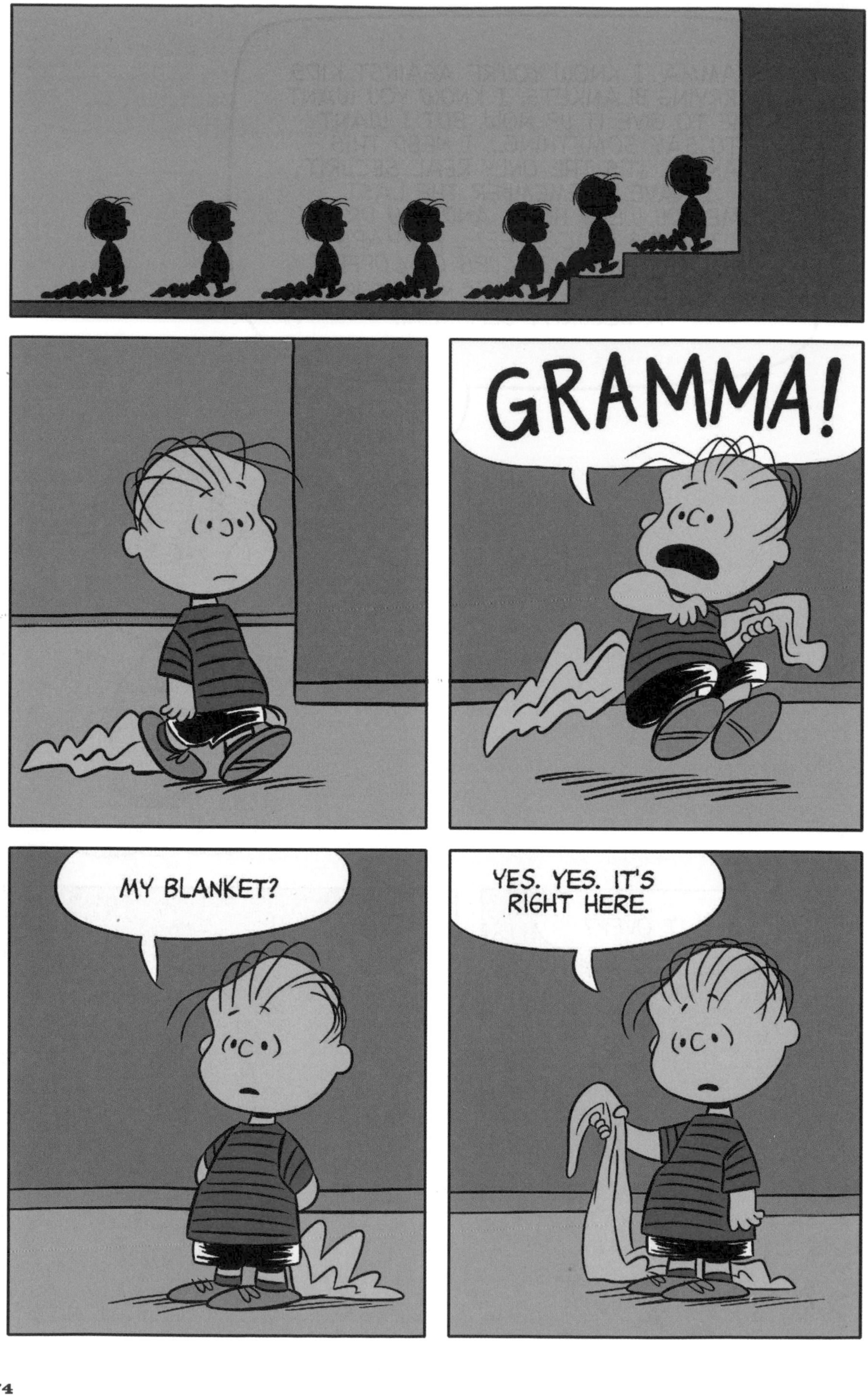
GRAMMA!
MY BLANKET?
YES. YES. IT'S RIGHT HERE.

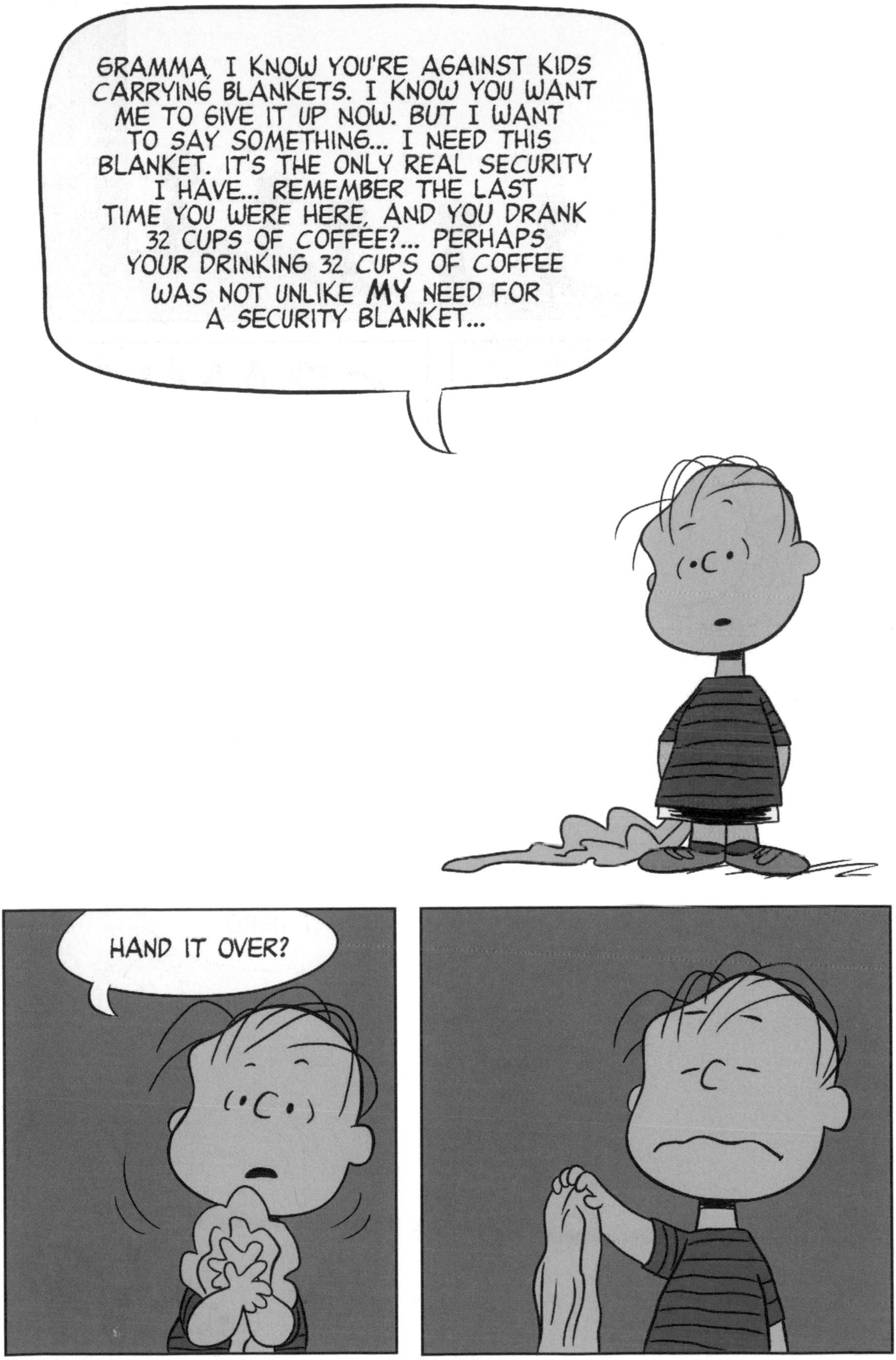
GRAMMA, I KNOW YOU'RE AGAINST KIDS CARRYING BLANKETS. I KNOW YOU WANT ME TO GIVE IT UP NOW. BUT I WANT TO SAY SOMETHING... I NEED THIS BLANKET. IT'S THE ONLY REAL SECURITY I HAVE... REMEMBER THE LAST TIME YOU WERE HERE, AND YOU DRANK 32 CUPS OF COFFEE?... PERHAPS YOUR DRINKING 32 CUPS OF COFFEE WAS NOT UNLIKE MY NEED FOR A SECURITY BLANKET...
HAND IT OVER?

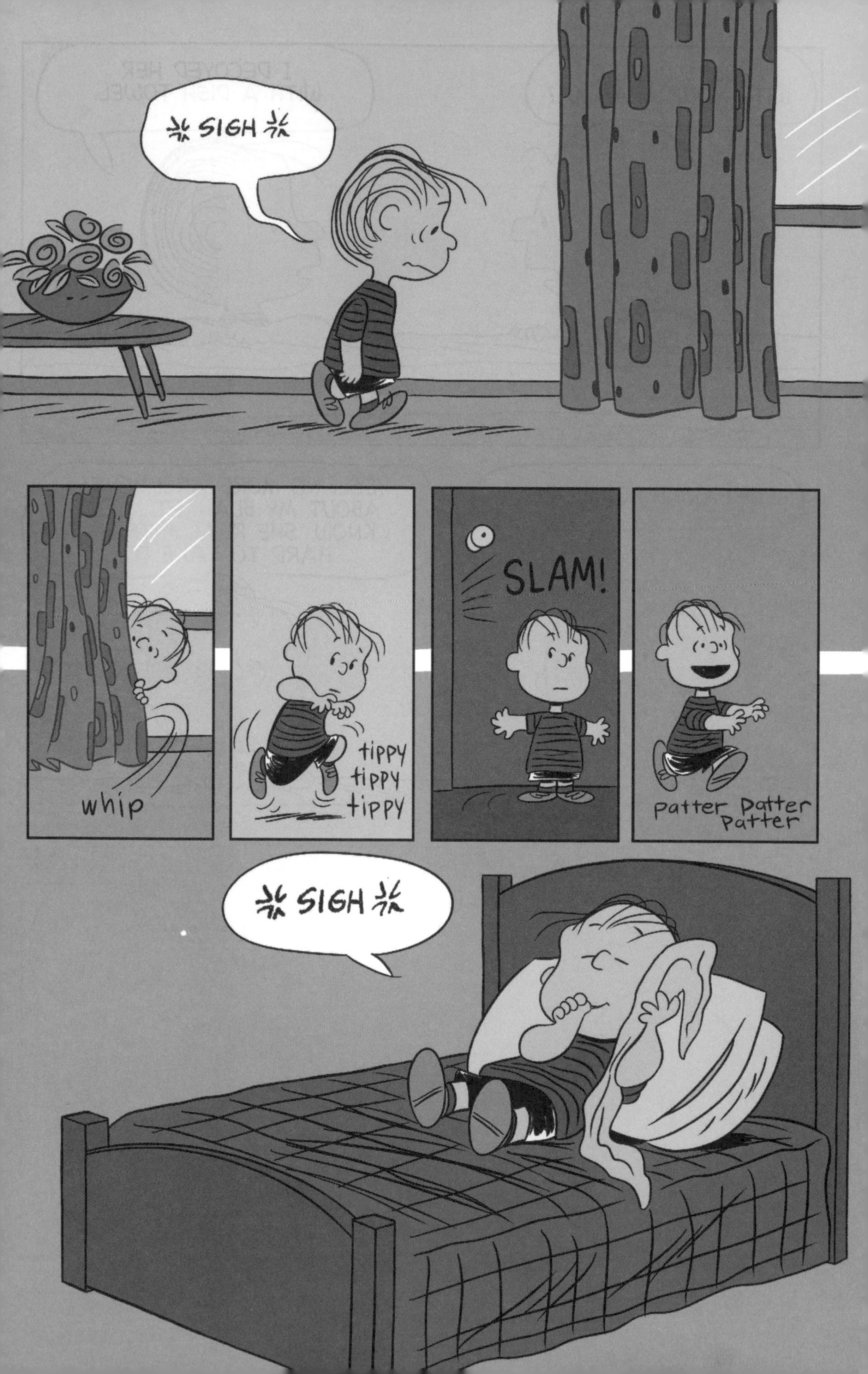
SIGH
whip
tippy
tippy
tippy
SLAM!
patter patter
patter
SIGH

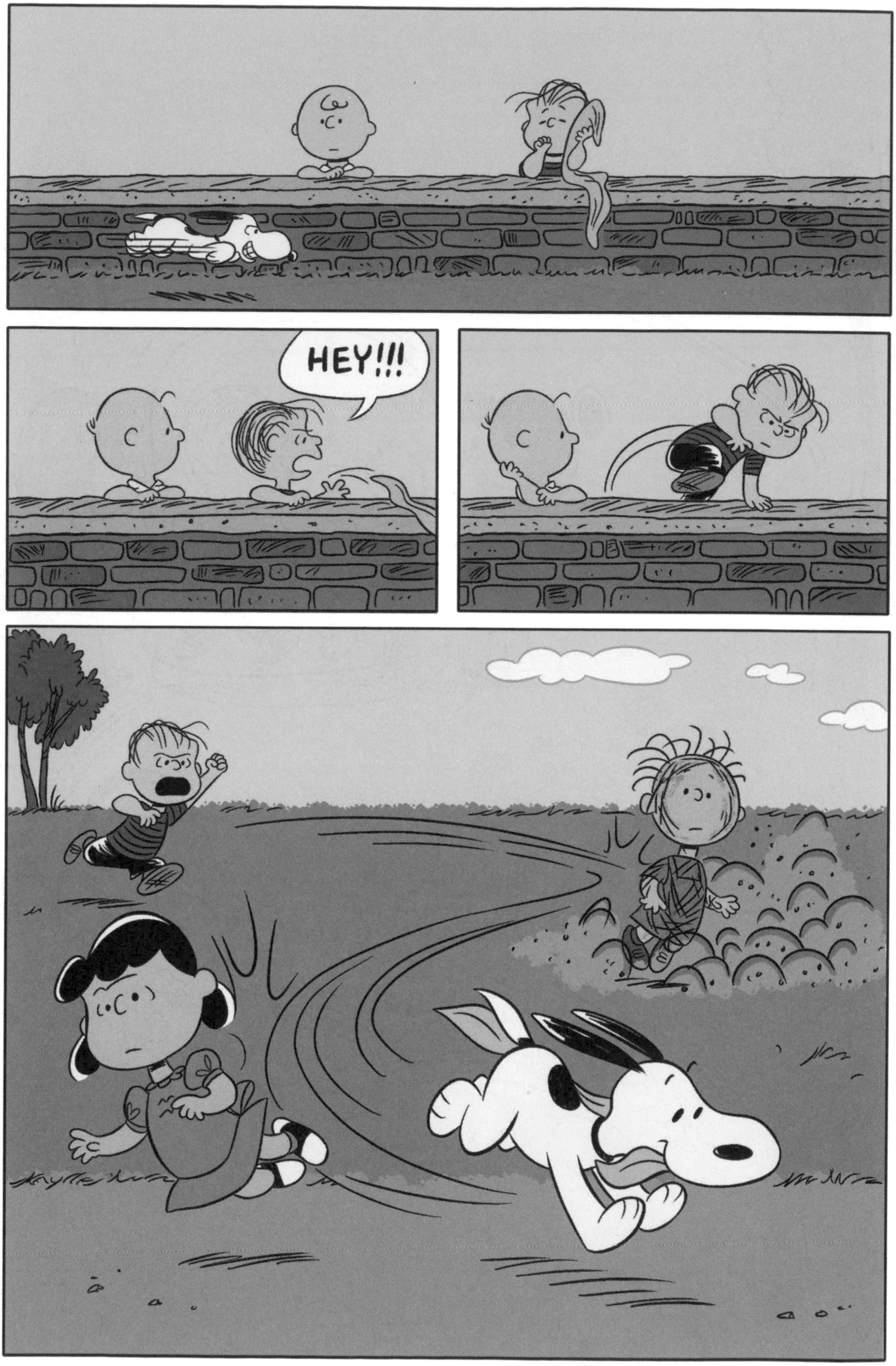
HEY!!!

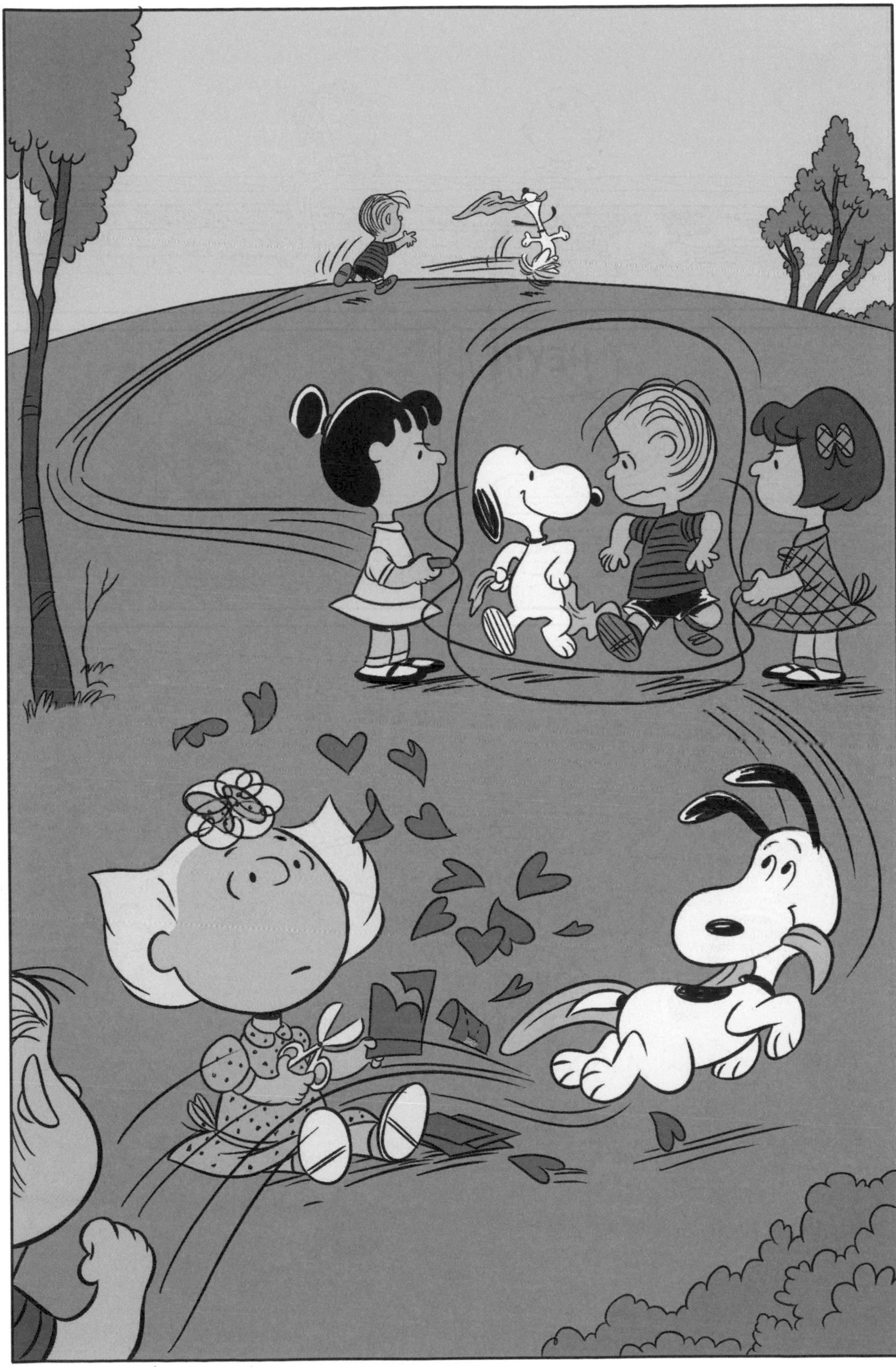

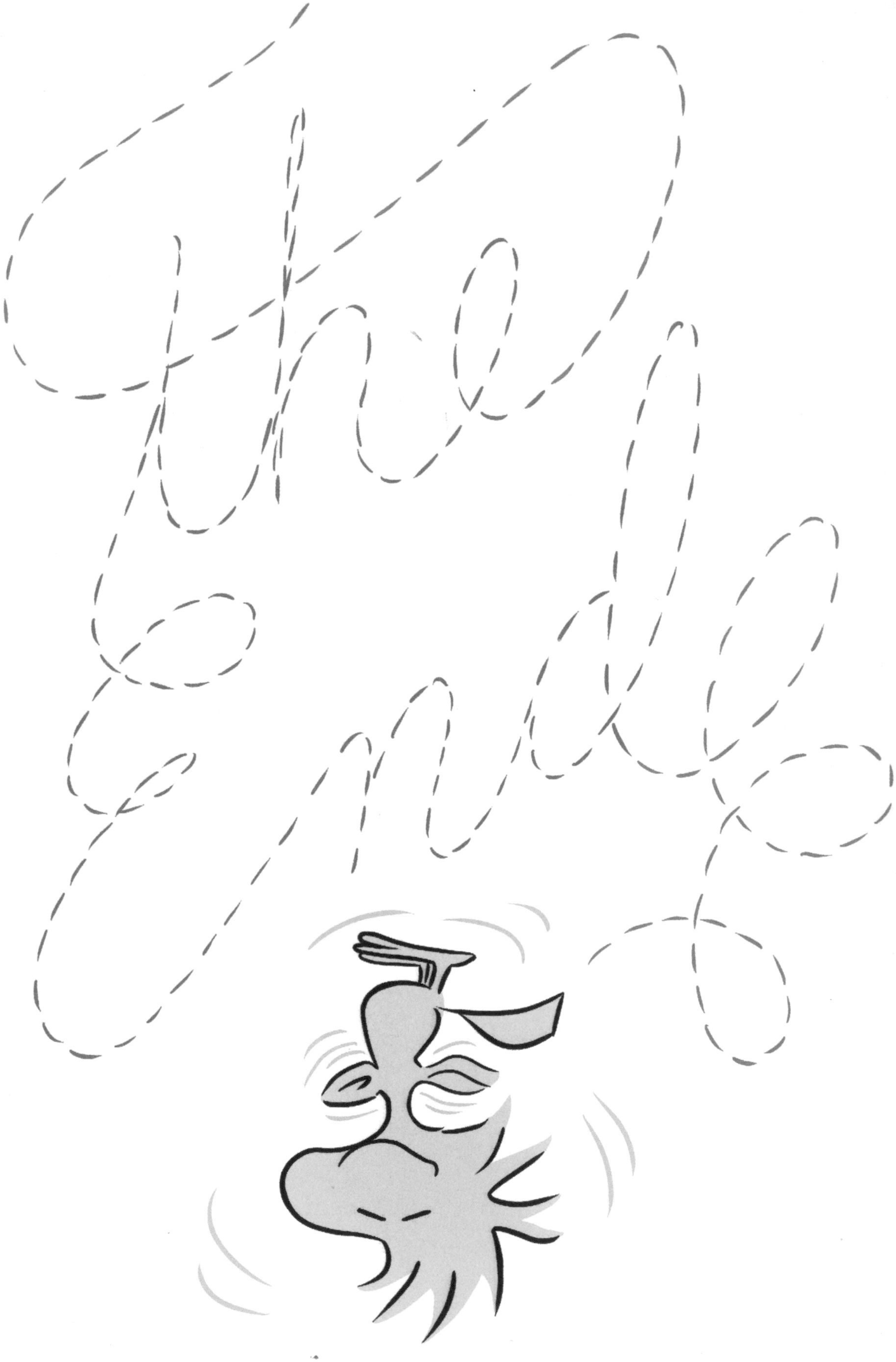
The End

BEHIND-THE-SCENES

Happiness
is a warm
Blanket
Charlie Brown.™

ANIMATED SPECIAL

Happiness is a Warm Blanket, Charlie Brown is the first all-new animated special from *Peanuts* in over five years. Adapted from Charles M. Schulz's comic strip, the story is centered on Linus and his security blanket woes. Directed by Andy Beall and Frank Molieri, the special is a throwback to some of the best *Peanuts* animated specials:

A Charlie Brown Christmas, It's the Great Pumpkin, Charlie Brown, and *Charlie Brown's All-Stars.*

The following model sheets, character poses and reference material was all part of the production on this newest *Peanuts* animated special.

CHARLIE BROWN LINUS SALLY WOODSTOCK LUCY SCHROEDER SNOOPY SHERMY PATTY VIOLET PIG-PEN

Above The cast of characters for *Blanket*; the look is derived from *Peanuts* comic strips circa 1963-64.

Above & Below Development sketches of Charlie Brown and Snoopy, by Andy Beall.

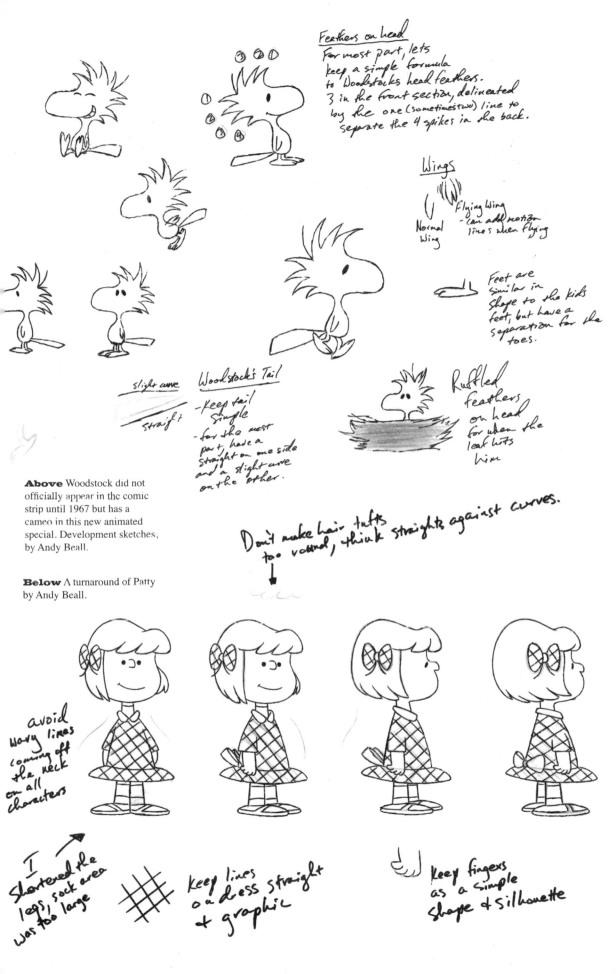

Feathers on head
For most part, lets keep a simple formula to Woodstocks head feathers. 3 in the front section, delineated by the one (sometimes two) line to separate the 4 spikes in the back.

Wings

Normal Wing

Flying Wing - can add motion lines when flying

Feet are similar in shape to the kids feet, but have a separation for the toes.

slight curve
straight

Woodstock's Tail
- Keep tail simple
- for the most part, have a straight on one side and a slight curve on the other.

Ruffled feathers on head for when the leaf hits him

Above Woodstock did not officially appear in the comic strip until 1967 but has a cameo in this new animated special. Development sketches, by Andy Beall.

Below A turnaround of Patty by Andy Beall.

Don't make hair tufts too round, think straights against curves.

avoid wavy lines coming off the neck on all characters

I shortened the legs, sock area was too large

keep lines and dress straight + graphic

keep fingers as a simple shape & silhouette

LINUS' HEAD CONSTRUCTION

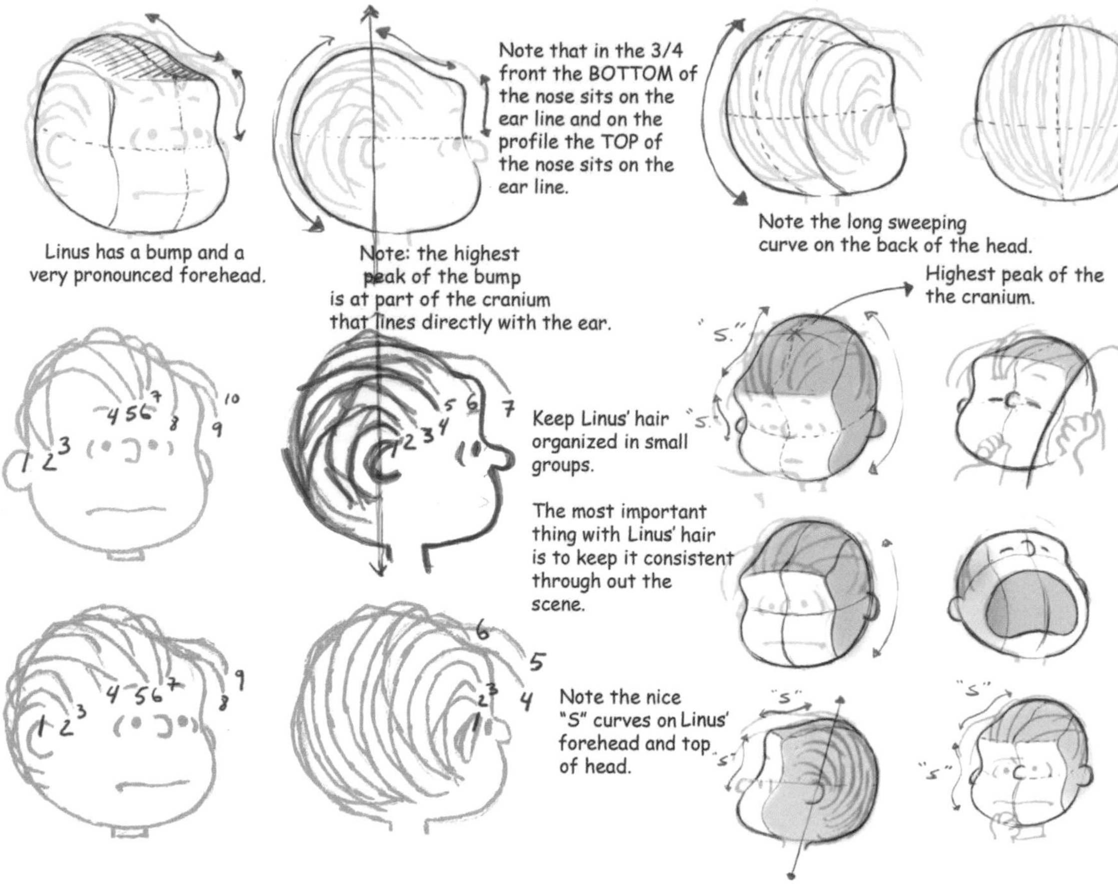
Note that in the 3/4 front the BOTTOM of the nose sits on the ear line and on the profile the TOP of the nose sits on the ear line.
Note the long sweeping curve on the back of the head.
Linus has a bump and a very pronounced forehead.
Note: the highest peak of the bump is at part of the cranium that lines directly with the ear.
Highest peak of the the cranium.
Keep Linus' hair organized in small groups.
The most important thing with Linus' hair is to keep it consistent through out the scene.
Note the nice "S" curves on Linus' forehead and top of head.

SHOES

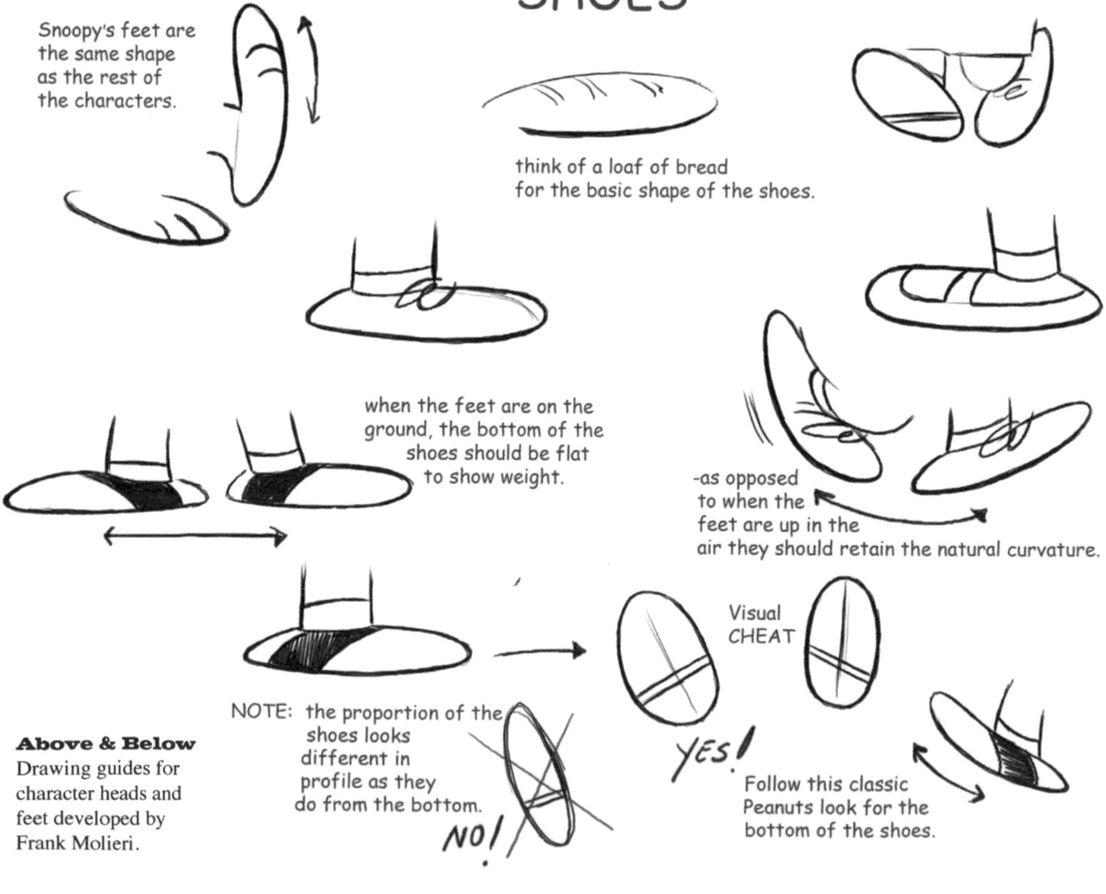
Snoopy's feet are the same shape as the rest of the characters.
think of a loaf of bread for the basic shape of the shoes.
when the feet are on the ground, the bottom of the shoes should be flat to show weight.
-as opposed to when the feet are up in the air they should retain the natural curvature.
Visual CHEAT
NOTE: the proportion of the shoes looks different in profile as they do from the bottom.
NO!
YES!
Follow this classic Peanuts look for the bottom of the shoes.

Above & Below
Drawing guides for character heads and feet developed by Frank Molieri.

Above Heads and feet in action! A blue-line penciled page by Bob Scott from the graphic novel adaptation.

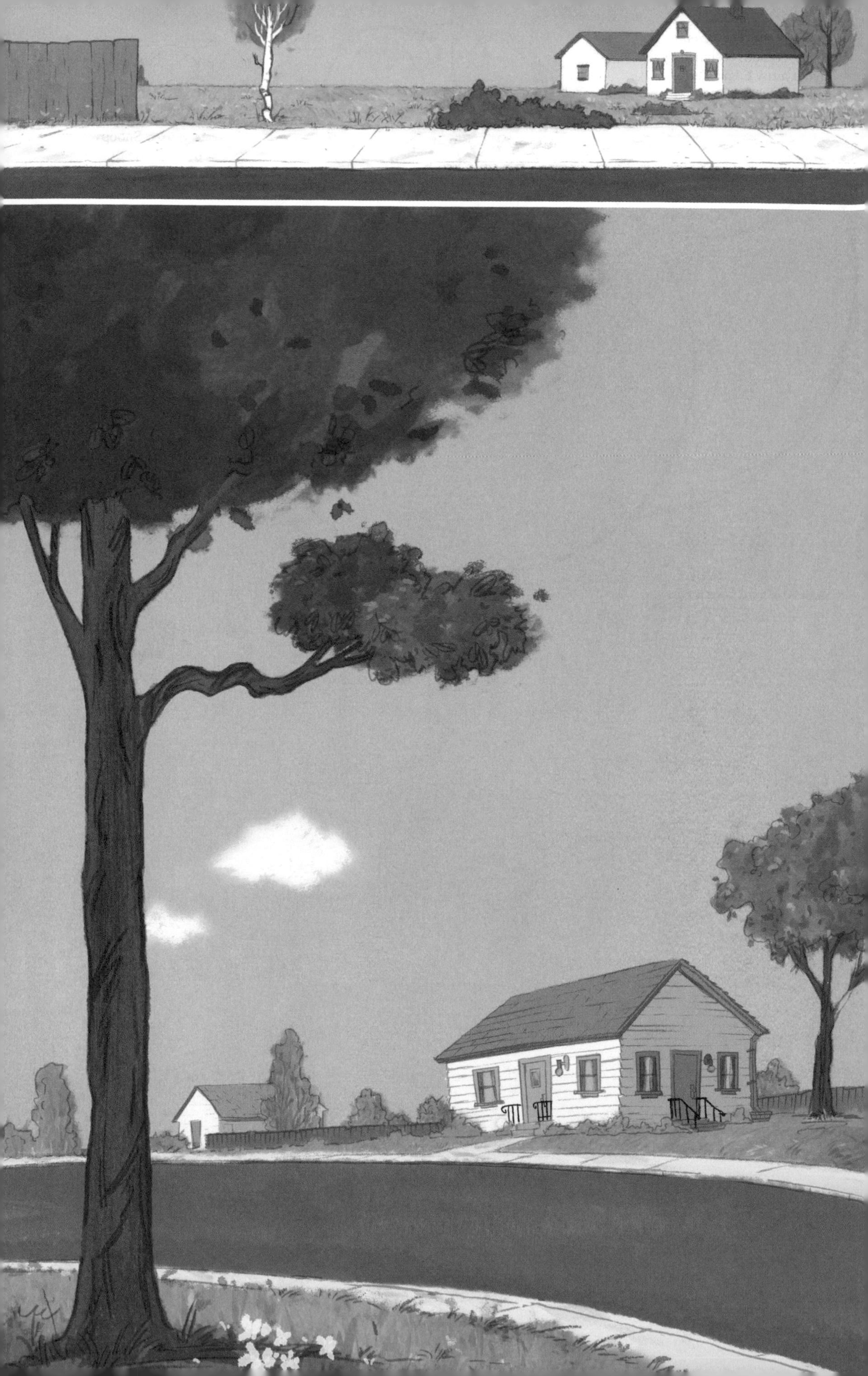

Opposite The *Peanuts* neighborhood: designed by layout artist Edgar Carlos and painted by Rozalina Tchouchev.

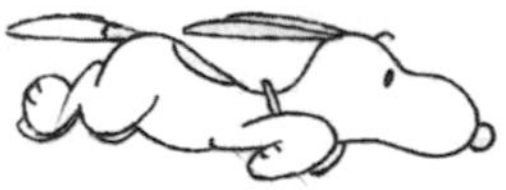

Above Snoopy, by Andy Beall.

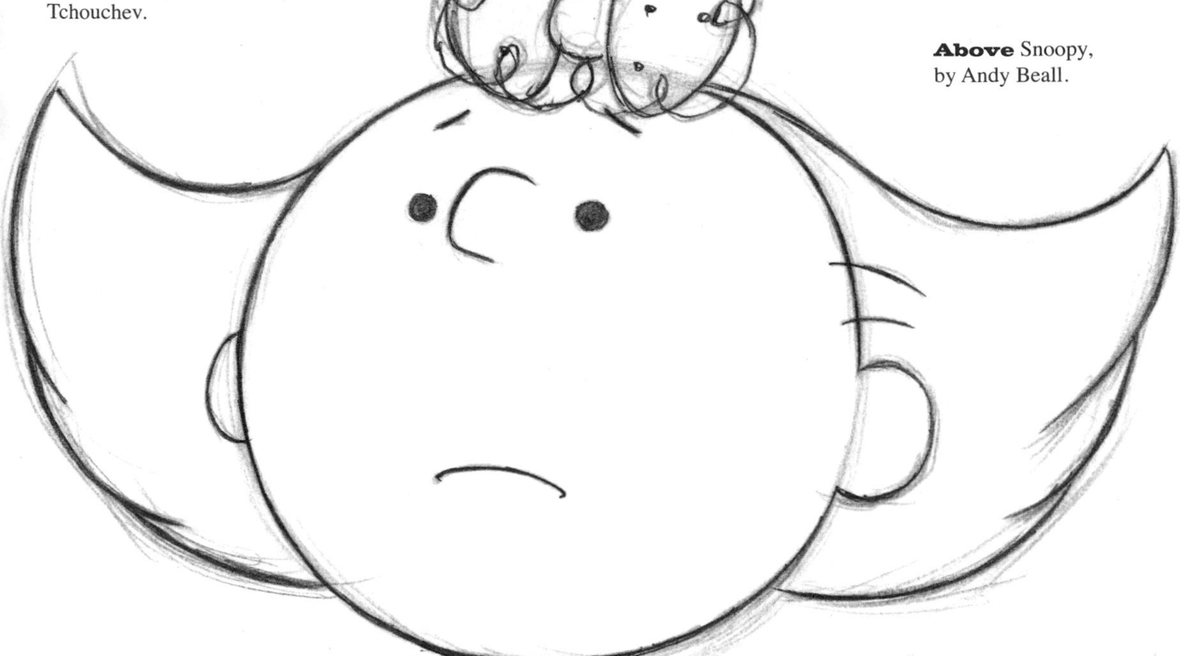

Above Sally looking at the stars, by Andy Beall.

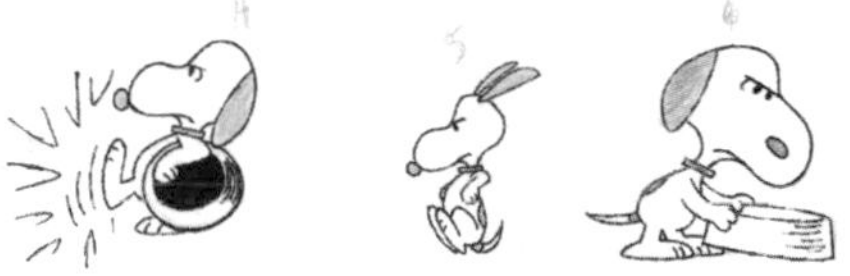

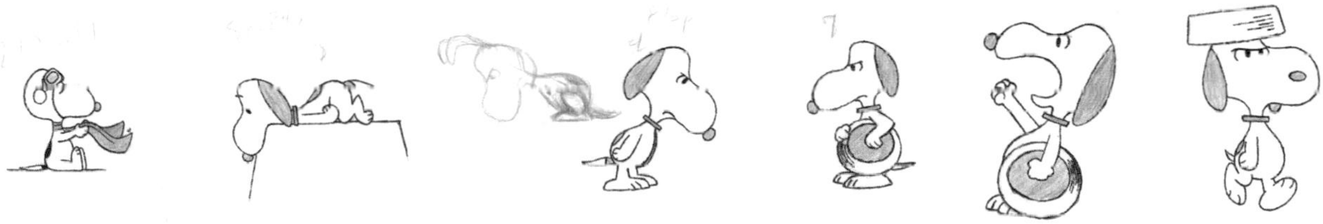

Above A variety of animation drawings of Snoopy, by Andy Beall.

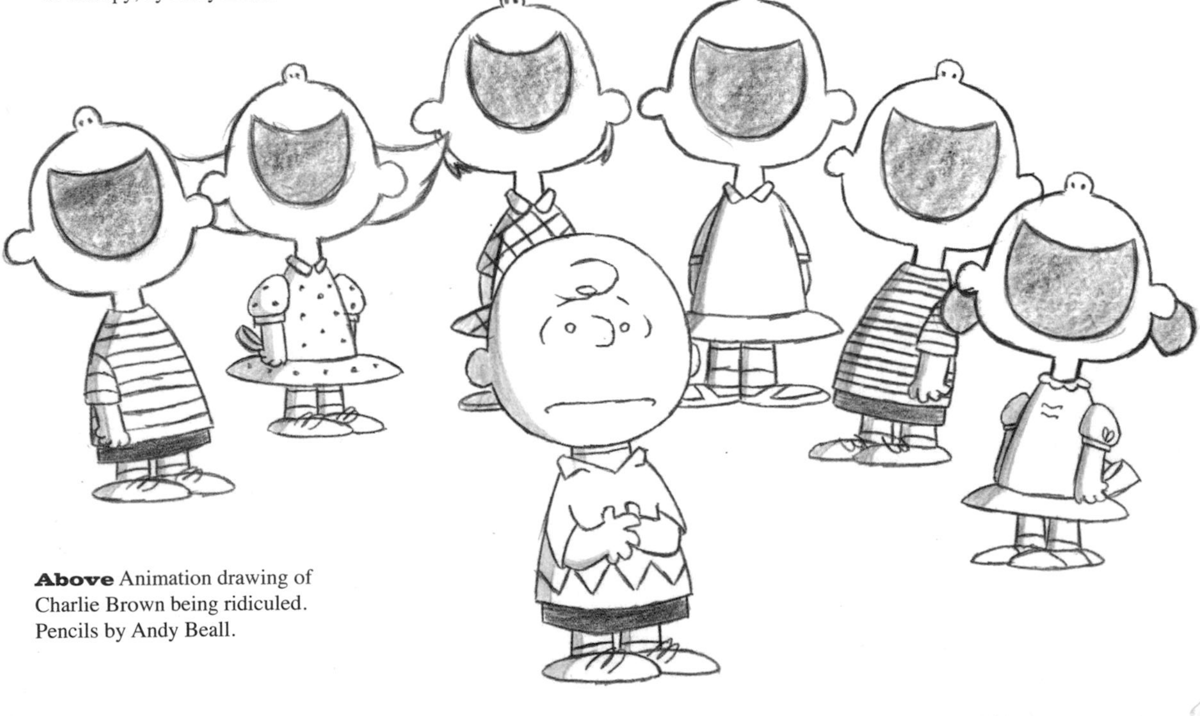

Above Animation drawing of Charlie Brown being ridiculed. Pencils by Andy Beall.

Above & Below Turnarounds of Lucy Van Pelt and Charlie Brown, by Andy Beall.

Opposite The *Peanuts* neighborhood: *(top)* layout by Edgar Carlos painted b Rozlina Tchouchev. *(below)* layouts by Edgar Carlos, painted by Seonna Hong.

Below Drawing guide by Frank Molieri.

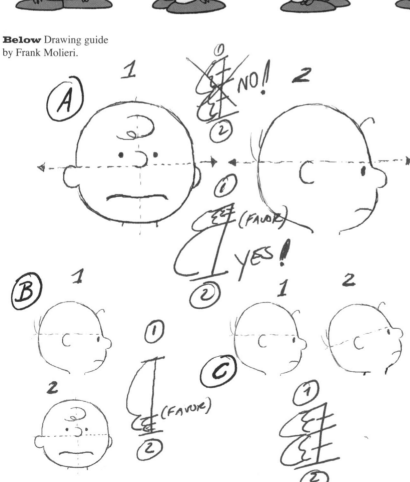

CONSTRUCTION AND TIMING NOTES:

NOTE:
On the 3/4 front the BOTTOM of the nose sits on the ear line and in a profile, the TOP of the nose sits on the ear line.

ALWAYS AVOID EVEN INBETWEENS OR THE FACE FEATURES WILL MORPH AND SLIDE UP AND DOWN FROM ONE POSE TO THE NEXT CAUSING

A RETAKE.

TIMING:

Always avoid even timing when there is a perspective change in the drawings as in samples A and B.

It's ok to do even timing when there is no perspective change in the drawings as in sample C.

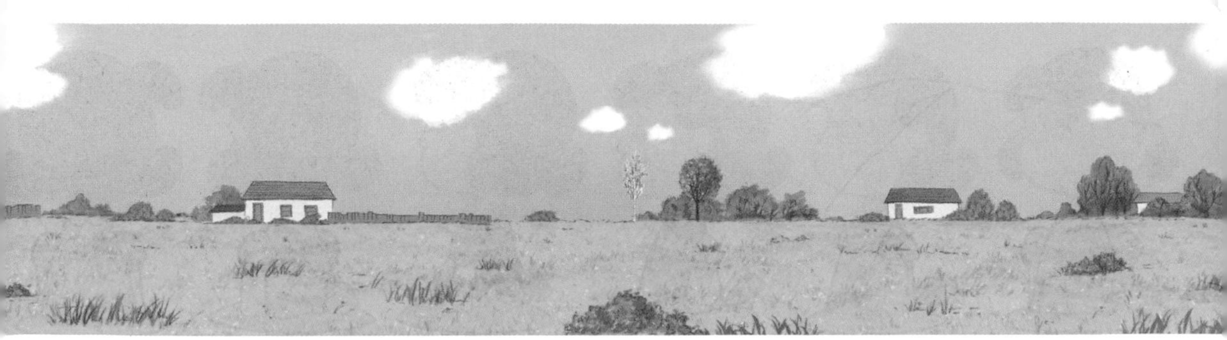

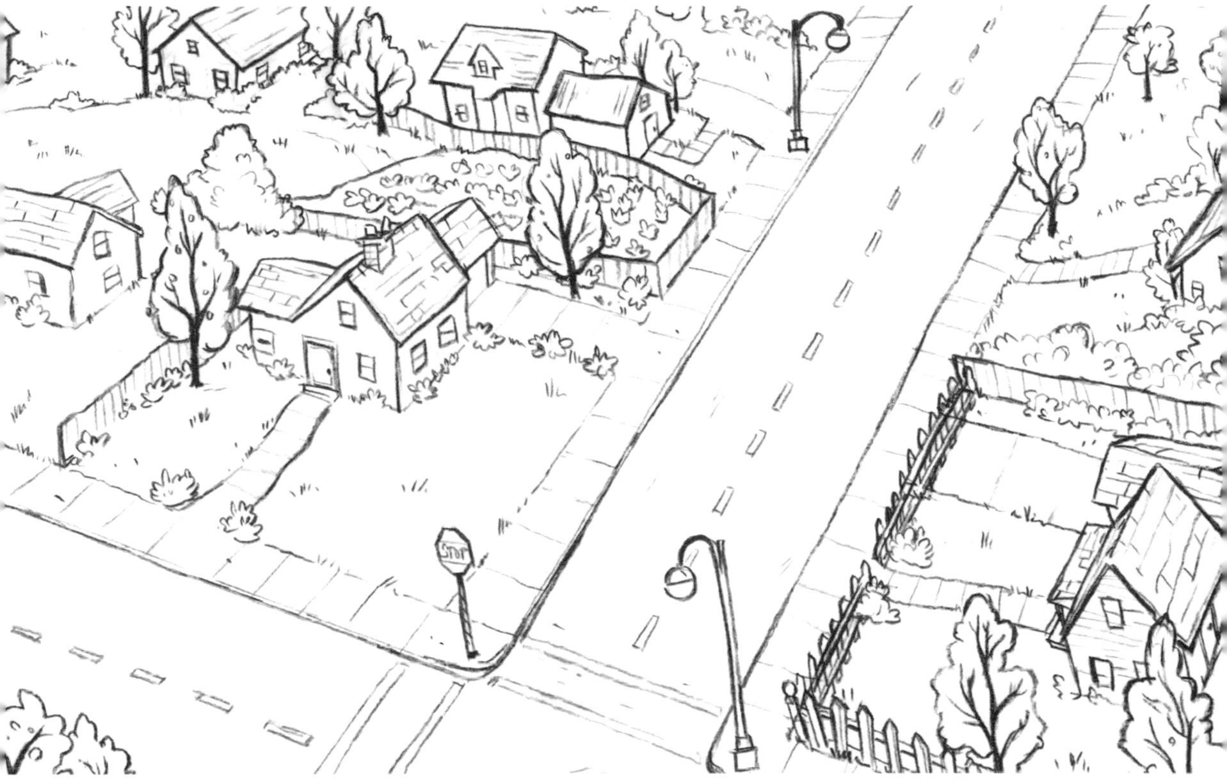
STOP

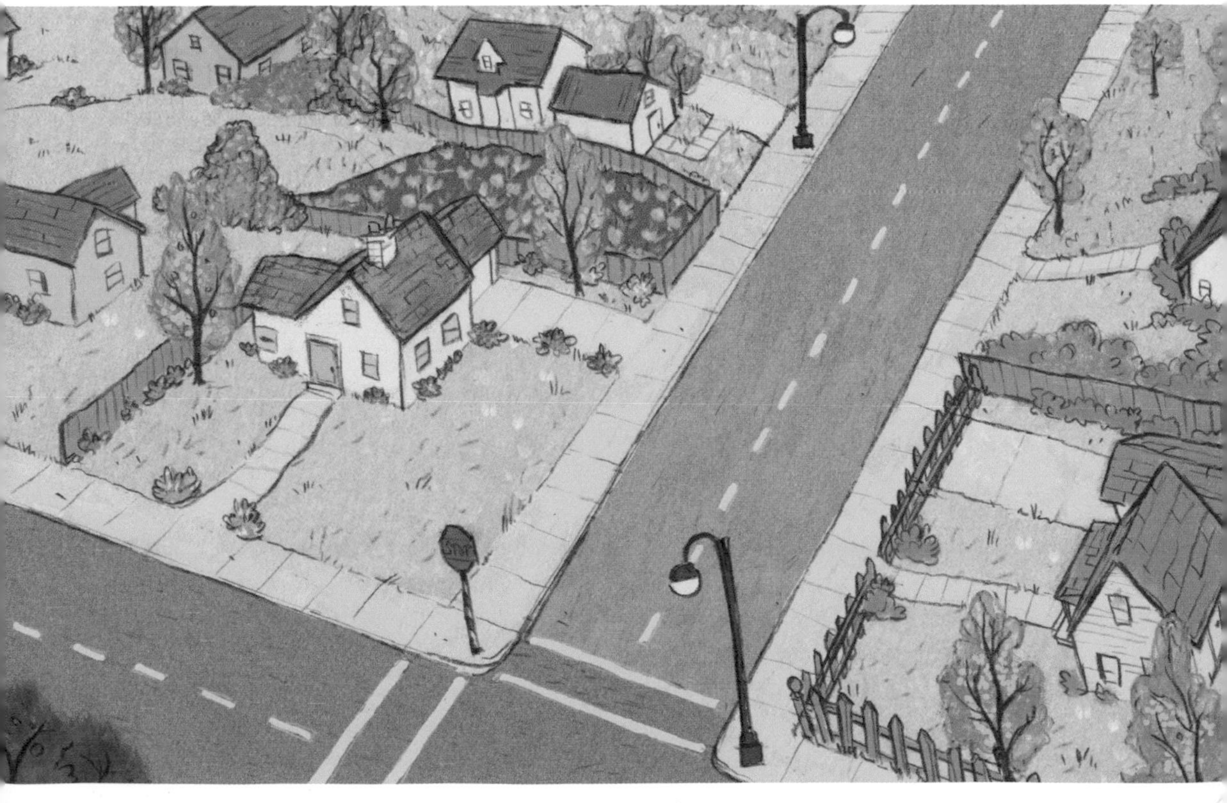

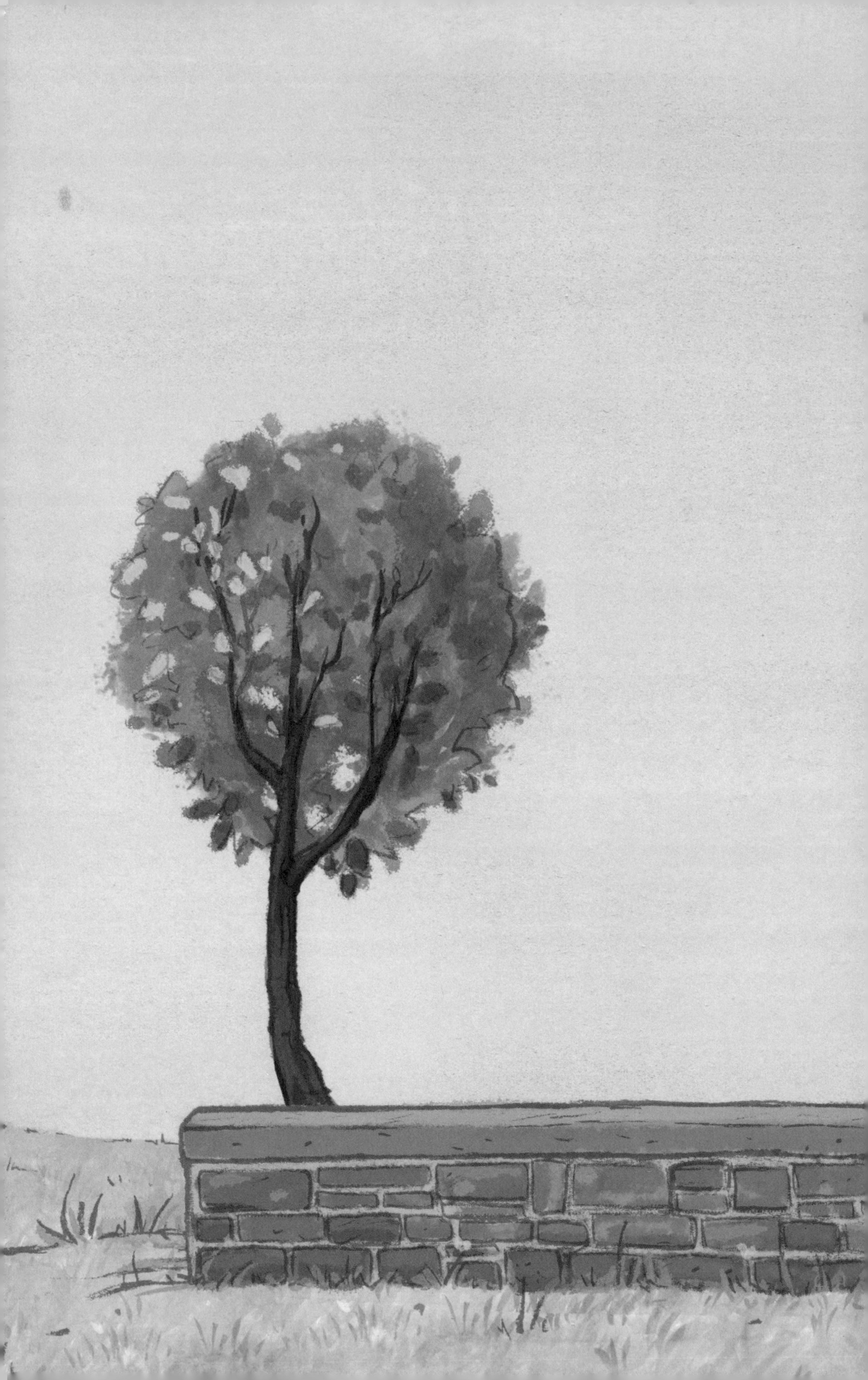

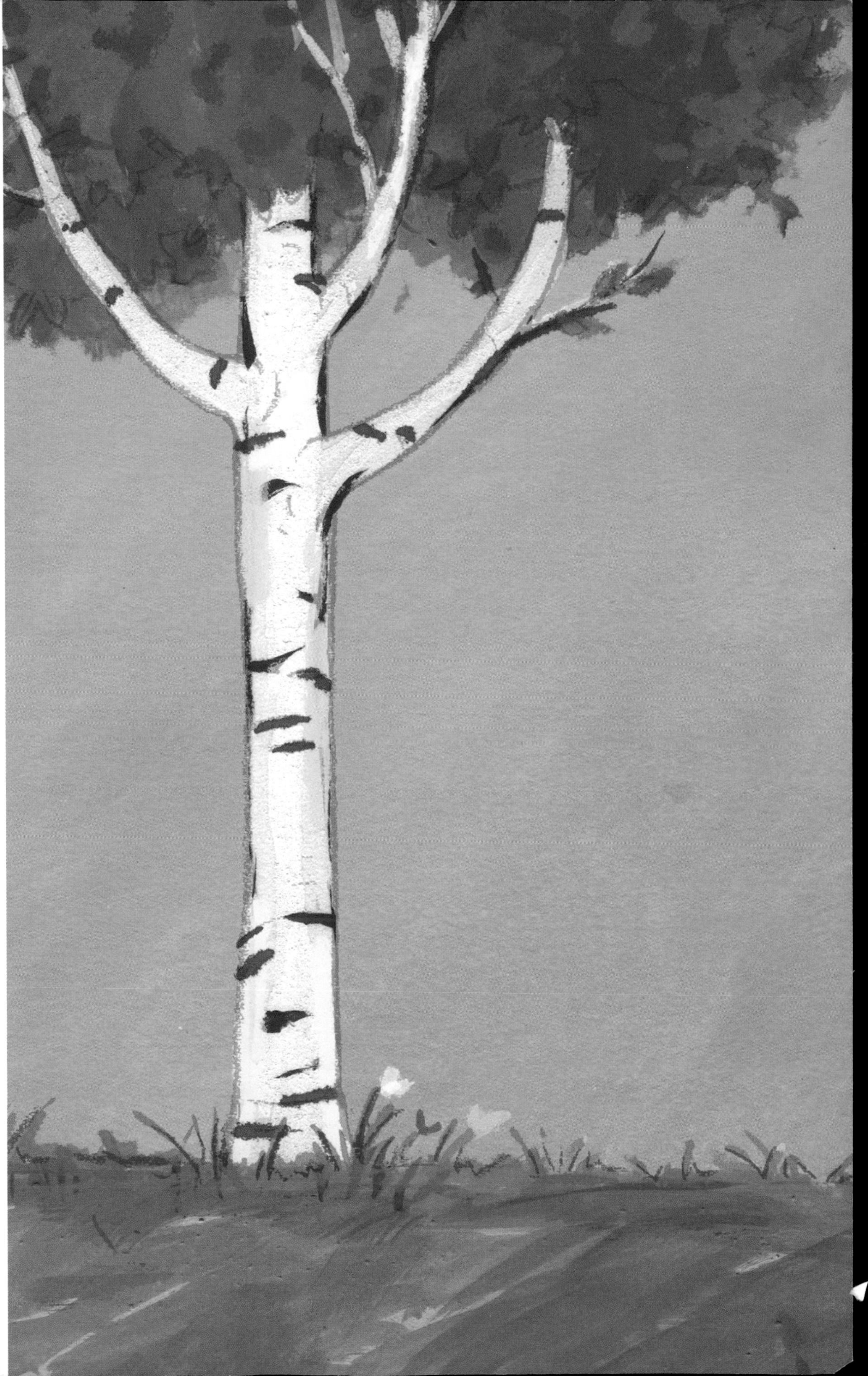

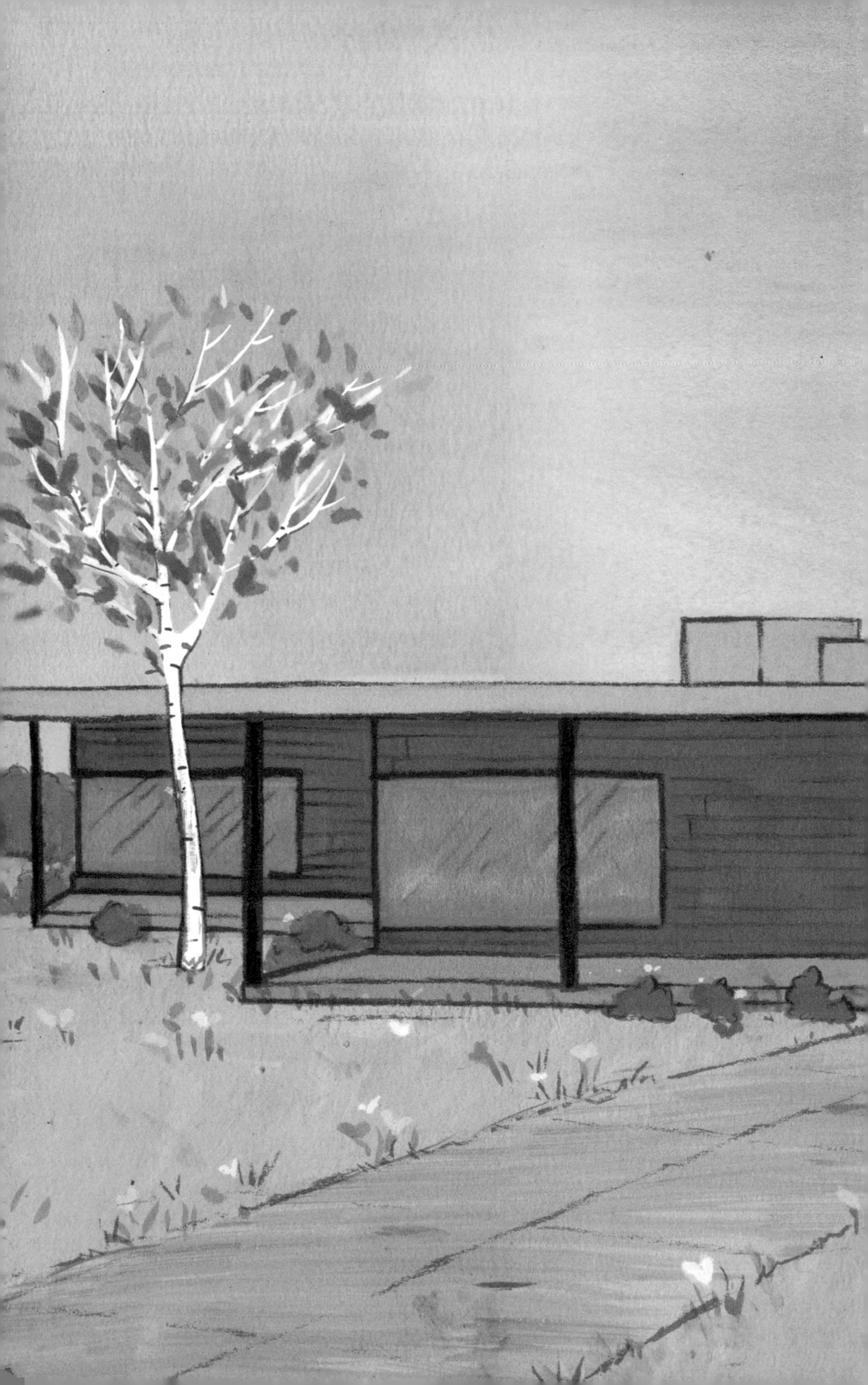